*The
Myth
of the
Greener
Grass*

J. Allan Petersen

TYNDALE HOUSE PUBLISHERS, INC.

The Myth of the Greener Grass

WHEATON, ILLINOIS

Second printing, April 1983

Library of Congress Catalog Card Number 82-50997
ISBN 0-8423-4656-2   HQ 806. P 48
Copyright © 1983 by J. Allan Petersen
Printed in the United States of America

C O N T E N T S

Is Anyone Faithful Anymore?

*What was once labeled adultery
and carried a stigma of guilt
and embarrassment
now is an affair—
a nice-sounding,
almost inviting word
wrapped in mystery,
fascination, and
excitement.*

OW COME you didn't finish the story?" he asked, shaking my hand as he left the late-morning session at the conference for men. I had told the story of a man whose unfaithfulness had ruined his own marriage, caused a divorce in another family, and left indelible scars on his children.

"What do you mean?" I inquired.

"Petersen, that story doesn't usually end in tragedy and disappointment; it's often through an extramarital affair that a person finds true love, happiness, and joy for the first time. Can we have lunch together?"

In the car, driving to the restaurant, I learned that this plain-looking middle-aged man was a minister, pastoring three small churches in the area. Although married to a beautiful and talented woman (his own description), he was deeply involved with a young pianist in one of his churches.

"My wife is a good woman, but when I married her, it was only an intellectual decision, and we didn't know what love was. Our marriage is solid, but not too exciting, and our three teen-aged children are getting along fine."

"Tell me about the pianist."

"I started making pastoral calls at her home when her children were at school and her husband was at work. I discovered we were compatible in so many ways, and there was an aliveness about her that my wife didn't have. I liked the way I acted and felt when I was with her. The first time we had sex together it was out of this world." With nervous excitement in his voice, he continued, "She is so uninhibited and fulfills every sexual fantasy I ever had. I hadn't ever had much fun in my life; I had never felt young, romantic, or sexy. For the first time I've discovered what real love is all about. We have a right to be happy, don't we? Anything this good has to be right. I would rather go to hell with her than to heaven with my wife."

"Real love?" I asked.

"Certainly! I am always looking out for her best interests. I would never hurt her. I wouldn't think of having intercourse with her while she was having her period or when she would be apt to get pregnant."

"If this is true love, why don't you divorce your wife and marry her?" I suggested, facetiously.

"What? You must be kidding! Why, that would be wrong. I don't want to hurt my wife and break up two families."

The Blonde
She was a strikingly attractive woman—young and somewhat shy. I had met her after a seminar session and she asked if I had time to hear her story. Immaculately dressed, her hair styled and sprayed so that not one strand wandered, she looked like a model on assignment. When we sat down, she was extremely careful of her posture. The position of her hands and feet was such that I assumed she was either very self-conscious or had been trained in a finishing school. Poised and carefully weighing every word, she recounted her disappointing marriage that was now on the verge of collapse. She and her husband had driven fifty miles to attend the seminar.

The checkered history of their marriage seemed to focus on one complaint: "I need so much for him to like me. I need to feel as though I mean something to him. I would give anything if just once he would say I am wonderful or beautiful to him. I can't understand why I get compliments from other people on my appearance or talents, but he doesn't seem to be aware of them at all."

"Have you found someone else who does encourage and

appreciate you?" I asked. She flinched, looked at the floor, and hesitatingly nodded her head. "Tell me about it."

"I know this is wrong, and I feel guilty about it, but I don't know what to do. I never intended to have an affair—in fact, this man is the homeliest man I know—but I have learned to love him. When I first met him he repulsed me, but he talked kindly and understandingly; he accepted me, made me feel like a woman—important, attractive—and gave me the emotional support I wanted so much from my husband. I ultimately forgot what he looked like, because when someone does this for you, you want to give him back so much more—everything you have."

By now there were tears in her eyes and she exclaimed, "I can't bear the thought of giving him up because I don't think my husband will ever change."

The Businessman

I was settled in my hotel room, waiting. There was a knock at the door; the man who had phoned for an appointment had arrived. He was well known in the city, successful in business, and highly regarded for his leadership ability and his fine marriage and family. He came from good stock, was educated in Christian schools—a leader in his church and actively involved in many Christian enterprises.

After we had exchanged pleasantries, he settled nervously in a chair. "How can I help you?" I asked. For several minutes he spoke in general terms of problems that are common to man: "Everyone faces problems . . . no one is perfect . . . even as Christians we often struggle with questions no one knows about . . . sometimes there are things inside which others cannot see, and things happen that surprise us. . . ."

I sensed his embarrassment in coming to the difficult point of revealing the purpose of his visit. He circled the problem repeatedly, looking for some hint of understanding in my eyes. Finally, in an effort to help him, I asked, "Why don't you just tell me what her name is and how it started?"

"Then you do know, don't you?" And, of course, then I did.

He described the recent misunderstandings he and his wife had had over the children and how their relationship had become strained. They were drifting apart. At this very time of loneliness he seemed unavoidably thrown together in church activities with an attractive and younger divorcée. She had been disappointed in her husband: "He was just plain dull, lethargic, no charisma—nice but dull." Their stories were like two missing pieces of a puzzle. They fit perfectly. It almost seemed providential, something thrust upon them by fate. They understood each other, needed each other. Eyes and hands touched—exhilaration, a spark, a flame, and before they knew it, they were in bed together.

At the time of our conversation, they had rendezvoused often, and he was struggling with the feelings of terror and fascination—love and a gnawing guilt. "I've always known something like this shouldn't be, but when it happens to you, it is different. I sincerely prayed that if God didn't want this in our lives, he would take away these feelings I have for her. We have even prayed together. I have prayed this over and over and He hasn't done it; therefore, it must mean He wants us together."

In a small midwestern town, the crowd was dismissed and the church was becoming empty and silent. One woman had lingered and asked if I had a moment. Rising right to the point, she expressed her strong disagreement with one part of my message. "You call it adultery; I call it an affair. You make it sound like the worst thing in the world. I am not involved with some dirty bum on the street. This man is respected and is as good as anybody in this church. This just happens to be my besetting sin—what's yours? You're no angel, are you?" She winked at me and went out into the night.

These are just four of the hundreds of men and women who have shared their marital secrets with me during my thirty-eight years of traveling ministry—pastors' wives, missionaries, Sunday school teachers, Christian counselors, church members, and much-used Christian leaders. They reflect the increasing incidence of extramarital affairs among professing Christian people, the broad range of people affected, and the tendency to find reasons to support our behavior, even though those reasons might be contrary to the moral and biblical convictions we have long held.

NO NEW PROBLEM

Infidelity within marriage is not a new idea. It is not a product of the so-called sex revolution or of the new morality. Extramarital affairs have been with us for thousands of years. "When the Pharaohs ruled Egypt," New York psychiatrist Alexander Wolf points out, "the husband's virtue, continence, and marital faithfulness were required of him, and his infidelity was dealt with harshly." Social scientist Robert A. Harper states that "regulations regarding extramarital intercourse and violations of those regulations are certainly buried in man's prehistoric past. All known cultures have some limitations set upon extramarital sex relations and some means of enforcing such designated taboos."[1] In one study by anthropologist J. S. Brown, it was found that among eighty-eight societies in various parts of the world, 89 percent of these groups punished their people when they were discovered to be party to an extramarital affair. In another study of 148 societies, taboos against extramarital affairs appeared in 81 percent of them.[2]

However, a call for fidelity in the '80s is like a solitary voice crying in today's sexual wilderness. What was once labeled adultery and carried a stigma of guilt and embarrassment now is an affair—a nice-sounding, almost inviting word wrapped in mystery, fascination, and excitement. A relationship, not sin. What was once behind the scenes—a secret closely guarded—is now in the headlines, a TV theme, a best seller, as common as the cold. Marriages are "open"; divorces are "creative."

Sexual promiscuity has never been the established custom in any human society, but always considered a negative influence on the family and society. Even *Playboy* magazine, hardly committed to strong marriages, discovered in a carefully selected survey that the *overwhelming majority* of both men and women were against extramarital sex for people in general and for themselves in particular.[3]

This is hardly in agreement with the father of "sex reporting," Dr. Alfred Kinsey. In 1953 he reported that half of the men and one-fourth of the women he surveyed acknowledged extramarital affairs. Every author since who writes on what the American male does relies frequently on these reports and builds on them. But Kinsey's reports were not accurate. He did not really sample the American male. Instead, of the "5,000 American men, a remarkably large part were in prisons, hospitals for mental diseases, institutions for the mentally deficient, homosexuals."[4] Hardly a representative group known for their stable moral and mental health.

Shere Hite, modern sex surveyor, says her findings reveal 66 percent of men have extramarital affairs. *McCalls* survey disagrees; it indicates only 16 percent. Other much-publicized statistics now agree with Hite, indicating that as many as two out of three husbands and close to one out of two wives have been unfaithful at some time during their marriage.

Of the 100,000 women respondents to the *Redbook* survey

of 1974, 30 of each 100—almost one-third—had had affairs with other men. And if a woman had had premarital sex, she was much more likely to have an affair. Twenty-six of the thirty had had premarital intercourse.

Among wives thirty-five to thirty-nine years old, 38 percent had been unfaithful. For wage-earning wives, the percentage jumped to 47 percent—almost half. As more wives enter the work force, affairs will increase accordingly. No wonder some sociologists and sex researchers predict that eventually half of all American wives will engage in extramarital sex.

According to *Redbook,* nonreligious wives are twice as likely as strongly religious wives to have sex with men other than their husbands.

All of this, in spite of another survey that showed that 86 percent of those questioned believe extramarital sex is always or almost always wrong. Another 11 percent feel that special circumstances must be considered. Fewer than 3 percent say infidelity is not wrong at all. What we say we believe and how we live are sometimes poles apart.

During the recent sex scandals that rocked Capitol Hill, Dr. Sam Janus, professor at New York Medical College, said, "A safe bet would be that nearly half of the members of Congress were involved in affairs outside of marriage."[5]

But whatever the accurate numbers, *Playboy's* "overwhelming majority" of people who are against affairs certainly don't control the media, movies, or advertising.

Sex, sex, sex. Our culture is near the point of total saturation. The cesspool is running over. Books, magazines, billboards, movies shout it ceaselessly. TV, the most powerful and immediate medium, trumpets it in living color. Sex gets the ratings. It is the recurring theme in daytime soaps and talk shows, the inevitable subject in the nighttime interviews. Every day, all day, the message bombards us like pellets from a brain-washing gun: "Get all the sex there is. All kinds. Anytime. You only go around once. Get all the gusto you can. Don't miss out. There is no tomorrow."

The Louis Harris-conducted study in 1978-79 polled 1,990 men between the ages of 18 and 49 and concluded that "the increased emphasis men are placing on self-fulfillment, pleasure, and doing one's own thing is dramatically altering America's traditional value system. The emerging self-oriented values represent a new personal liberalism. It is not a form of the old social liberalism. It stands apart from the traditional conservative-radical distinction based on social and economic issues. Its concern is for the conduct of one's personal life."[6]

Translate this philosophy to marriage and it says, "Fidelity is out; affairs are in." If your marriage does not provide at all times all you've ever expected, dreamed, or fantasized, and fails to bring you the constant sensory pleasure and fulfillment you deserve, find it elsewhere, enjoy some "healthy adultery." People are free spirits and shouldn't be pinned down. There must be no regulations on relationships.

"Healthy adultery" is the exact phrase used by Dr. Albert Ellis, prominent sexologist. He urged couples whose romantic love had faded from their marriage that adultery could be a healthy thing to rejuvenate their relationship. No suggestions on how to invigorate the relationship from within—how to build love again. Just a self-centered answer: go outside; have an affair.

All this pseudoscientific, pseudoliberated hoopla about the necessity of extra sex has done more than put more couples in bed. It has created a social climate that has bred fear and silence. The married faithful are less vocal than the unfaithful, as though fidelity, not infidelity, needs the defending in our sex-obsessed society. One working girl told me, "I work in an office with twenty-three other wives. I am the only one still faithful to my husband. They think I'm odd—ask me what my problem is."

Author Eva Baguedor in "Is Anyone Faithful Anymore?" tells about faithful women who seem self-deprecatory. They apologetically protest, "I'm midvictorian, I'm a square, I'm straight, and there's nothing interesting about that."

One wife volunteered, "I was at lunch last week with eleven women. We've been studying French together since our children were in nursery school. One gal, the provocateur of the group, asked, 'How many of you have been faithful throughout your marriage?' Only one woman at the table raised her hand. That evening my husband looked crestfallen when I told him I was not that one.

"'But I have been faithful,' I assured him.

"'Then why didn't you raise your hand?'

"'I was ashamed.'"[7]

That's like a person's being ashamed of his health during an epidemic, or apologizing for his vitality and energy at a crippled citizens' convention.

Though extramarital sex is more glamorized and more available than ever, are the results as positive as the promotion? We used to talk of the guilt, the pain, the assassination of self-esteem and the self-deceit of cheating. Have these disappeared with the kerosene lamp and can life now be one big sexual orgy with no problems, no regrets, no reverberations?

Medical doctors Alexander Lowen and Robert J. Levin chorus a resounding NO. Because of their unusual insights, I quote freely.

Consider, for example, a husband who is having sexual relations with another woman. His attitude, shared by many people in similar circumstances, is that sex and love are two different things, and that he has a right to enjoy sex as he would any of life's physical pleasures. But he loves and respects his wife; he values his marriage; he cherishes his children. As he sees it, his responsibility lies in protecting his family from any knowledge of his infidelities. Then, he argues, his wife loses nothing. She may even gain, because he returns to her a more loving and relaxed man. And so, in the name of love, he deceives her.

There are at least three ways in which infidelity can be disastrous to the future of any marriage. First, it inevitably causes pain to the other. *A marriage exists when a man and woman are bound together not by law but by love, and are openly pledged to accept responsibility for each other, fortified by the feeling of total commitment that extends from the present into the future. Virtually all such marriages begin with faith—which is to say that when a man and a woman entrust themselves to each other, they do so believing that neither would ever try to hurt the other, that each will contribute to the other's happiness, and that together they will seek fulfillment.*

The first breaking of that faith, the basic infidelity precedes *any act of extramarital intercourse. It happens when one partner decides to turn away from his mate in search of intimacy or fulfillment—and keeps the decision a secret. This is the true betrayal of trust. A man cannot or will not talk to his wife about matters that concern him deeply—and then discusses these concerns with another woman whose company he enjoys. He must keep the relationship a secret, because it would wound his wife to know the truth—and this, in turn, reinforces their separation.*

Also, the sexually unfaithful husband must devote time and money, as well as physical and emotional energy, to the other woman. Whatever he gives her, in effect, he must take from his wife. It means the wife is paying for his pleasures.

Second, infidelity masks the real problem. *To whatever extent infidelity temporarily eases the superficial symptoms of discontent in a husband or wife—such as feeling unattractive or unappreciated—it camouflages the real malady and permits it to grow worse. Instead of seeking an honest confrontation, with all its risks and promises, both accept the dishonesty of infidelity—in most cases, one actively, the other passively. Distressed by the thought of a separation or divorce, they pretend to be faithful while they search for satisfaction outside marriage.*

All too often it is the healthier and stronger member of the marriage who finds fulfillment elsewhere and then asks for a divorce. This leaves the other partner with a feeling of helplessness, and in a far worse position than if there had been a confrontation.

Third, it is destructive of the self. *The unfaithful partner who pretends that by keeping his affairs a secret he protects his wife and safeguards his marriage practices the deepest deception of all: self-deceit. Since the use of deceit transforms the person against whom it is used into an adversary, a self-deceived person is obviously his own worst enemy.*

As with all living creatures, we spontaneously reach out for pleasure and withdraw from pain. Telling the truth is a way of reaching for the pleasure of intimacy, as lovers well know. Telling a lie is an attempt to avoid punishment or pain. Therefore, it is natural to want to tell the truth in situations of trust and to lie in situations of danger.

It is when we feel we must lie to someone who trusts us and whom we love that we are trapped in what psychologists call a double bind. Whatever we do, we lose. This is what an unfaithful husband faces when he returns home to a wife he genuinely loves. He wants to restore his sense of closeness with her, but he knows he cannot tell her what he has done. So he lies.

But this lie has a boomerang effect. Instead of bringing him closer to his wife, it leaves him feeling farther away from her. The lie that spared him from her anger and rejection brought with it a pain of its own. In such situations, the stronger a person's desire to be close to the one he is deceiving, the greater the pain over the lie that divides them.

However, the person who does not care strongly about anything or anyone can, by tailoring his idea of love to suit his needs, tell both wife and mistress that he loves them—and believe it. The lies are unconscious, and therefore, not marked by pain. This is the ultimate act of self-deception. Instead of resolving conflict, it perpetuates it; the deluded person lives a lie. He is sick and does not feel the fever.[8]

So, there is pain, affecting everyone involved. There is something destructive about an affair—destroying one's inner integrity, a partner's self-esteem, and the possibility of intimacy, and it reverberates through future generations, affecting our children and theirs. The stolen melons eaten in secret are really poisonous.

The law of the harvest remains inexorable. Men break themselves over it but the law is never broken. "Don't delude yourself into thinking God can be cheated: where a man sows, there he reaps: if he sows in the field of self-indulgence he will get a harvest of corruption out of it; if he sows in the field of the Spirit he will get from it a harvest of eternal life."[9]

Doctors Lowen and Levin conclude:

The ultimate goal lies beyond being truthful with oneself. It consists of being faithful *to oneself. The person who is faithful to himself cannot live happily unless the twin strands of sex and love are woven together in his life. Because he is an undivided person, he seeks to be faithful to the woman he loves. His is the fidelity of love, not fear; of choice, not chance; of fulfilled desire, not extinguished feeling.*

CHAPTER 2

Rooftop Romance

*No good Christian man
or woman gets up in the morning,
looks out the window, and says,
"My, this is a lovely day!
I guess I'll go out
and commit adultery."
Yet many do it anyway.*

Florence Littauer

HE was an unusually beautiful woman of nineteen years, four years married, no children. For a few months now her middle-aged husband had been out of town on military duty. One spring evening, quite late, she was preparing to retire. She undressed for her bath. Her long, lustrous dark hair fell around her face and body, a picture of fresh feminine loveliness. The moon shone in upon her and highlighted her shapely form. She finished her private evening ritual of washing.

Roberta Kells Dorr described the scene graphically in her novel *David and Bathsheba.*

Bathsheba pulled off her shift and stepped into the alabaster bowl her servant Sarah had filled with fresh water. She stood naked in the bowl while her servant dipped water with a gourd and poured it over her. Bathsheba stood without embarrassment even though she had nothing to cover her nakedness. Unknown to her, a man's eyes had been observing and . . . ordinarily he would have turned away, but it was all so unexpected and lovely that he continued to watch. With growing admiration, he studied her loveliness as only half-seen through the dried palm branches. Her hair clung in damp curls to her full breasts and her tiny waist accentuated the pleasing roundness of her hips. As he watched, she stepped out of the bowl and tossed her hair back, making the curve of her back visible. He thought he'd never seen anything so beautiful or so graceful in his life.[1]

A quiet knock at her door totally changed her plans for the rest of that night and the rest of her life.

An extramarital affair. How does it start; what keeps it going; what are its characteristics; and who are, at the same time, its perpetrators and its victims?

The Bible never glosses over or omits human failure. God doesn't write human biographies as a doting father. The flaws and foolishness of His leaders are as clearly identified as their successes. No whitewash job. Their histories show that today's temptations are as old as man and that failure is a part of each of us. Now, of course, each story of marriage infidelity is different in many details: the geographical, social, and family setting—the age, attitudes, and background of the people involved. But the basic elements are the same, especially among professing Christians. And the account of David and Bathsheba is as modern as today's TV serial.

THE CIRCUMSTANCES

That spring day in Jerusalem was ordinary by all standards. There is nothing in the biblical record to indicate there was anything unusual about the day's activities or atmosphere. The shopkeepers hawked their wares as they had done for centuries; children played in the corridors of the old city, and the synagogues rang with the oft-repeated prayers of the people. Israel had just come through a series of battles with the Syrians and was enjoying the fruits of its victories. Peace and prosperity reigned. David, seeking to extend the boundaries of his kingdom, had sent his armies out to engage and destroy the Ammonites. Otherwise it was business as usual. Everything needed to keep that ancient city throbbing and its century-old traditions thriving was undisturbed.

No one suspected anything disastrous on this ordinary day, least of all David and Bathsheba. Nothing would indicate the frightening string of events spawned on that day—adultery, pregnancy, deception, murder, family tragedy, and divine judgment. All on just an ordinary day.

"I never dreamed this could happen to us," sobbed a pastor's wife in my office. "Things seemed to be going along all right, everything was normal, there were no foreboding signs—our church was growing, then—and it was so unexpected, so shocking. My husband asked for a divorce, resigned his church, and took up with this floozy woman who had been married three times already."

"All right," "normal," "no signs," "church growing," "unexpected." These are not words of surprise. Everything seems fine. No reason to suspect tragedy. The work is going well. God seems to be working. The family is settled. And then, without warning—the bombshell!

Joseph, in his early twenties, had great responsibility in Potiphar's household. He handled all his employer's domestic matters and business affairs. Everything was running smoothly—the crops flourishing, the flocks multiplying. This handsome young man had complete administration over everything without a worry in the world. God was prospering him.

Then one day—nothing special—while he was "going about his work," a woman began making eyes at him, seductively suggesting, "Joseph, come sleep with me!"

Upon arising that morning, Joseph would never have dreamed that the day—another ordinary working day—would bring him a passionate invitation to an affair, blackmail, and prison.

I, too, was unsuspecting. I had just arrived in a Michigan town to begin a series of meetings in the church on Sunday. It was a small, colorless community, common people, no sophistication. At this Saturday night get-acquainted reception, a church woman sat down beside me. She was far from glamorous or fashionable. A Plain Jane: no scintillating personality, slightly overweight, a common, everyday housewife type.

For a moment we exchanged pleasantries. Then in a matter-of-fact way she handed me a piece of paper with her address and phone number.

"I thought you might get lonely while you're here. If you'd

like to drop over some afternoon, give me a call. My husband is gone all week, working in Detroit. The last speaker we had at the church came over several times; I think you might enjoy it." Nothing subtle or sultry, cunning or coy—just as casual as offering a drink of water and with seemingly no more serious consequences.

Affairs don't begin on days with red lights of warning blazing. The day doesn't start out with dark, ominous clouds, tornado warnings, an inner restlessness, or a voice from heaven that says, "Double your defenses; temptation is coming." The tornado that destroyed my office building several years ago came unexpectedly on a lovely spring day, roared through like a 747, and left everything twisted, broken, and in shambles. And spring continued. So comes temptation. When? On any ordinary day.

THE CHARACTERS

I believe this affair came as something of a surprise to both David and Bathsheba. Neither one had planned for this an hour before it happened. It was not the result of flirtation or lecherous conniving. David was a man after God's own heart and Bathsheba was a faithful wife to her courageous and patriotic husband. David was just coming off a season of prosperity and fame. In numerous battles he had been victorious; he had destroyed 87,000, captured 22,000. And all these victories were confirmations of God's presence within him and of God's promise to give him an eternal dynasty. "So the Lord gave him victories wherever he turned."[2]

God's promises had just been uttered: "I chose you; I have been with you. You will become one of the most famous men in the world. Your family shall rule my kingdom forever." And David responded with overwhelming thanks: "Why have you showered your blessings on me? Such generosity is far beyond any human standard. You have done great miracles; may you be eternally honored. You are indeed God, your words are true."[3]

He had just previously gone out of his way to keep his vow to Jonathan and had restored to his heirs all the land formerly owned by Saul. Jonathan's lame son was invited to live at the palace as one of David's own family. Unashamedly, David had danced before the Ark of the Lord in the sight of the whole city in celebration, in praise of God. "I am willing to act like a fool in order to show my joy in the Lord," he said.[4] "David reigned with justice . . . and was fair to everyone."[5] So here's David, a man of great courage, generosity, and kindness, just and fair in his dealings, committed to God and full of praise and thanksgiving. Hardly a candidate for a personal disaster.

INNOCENT

To all appearances, both David and Bathsheba were innocent. Neither was engaged in any activity that could be interpreted as encouraging infidelity or compromise. Bathsheba was involved in the innocent task of taking an evening bath. Nothing sensual here. She wasn't parading her feminine charms, seeking to entice. Neither cheap streetwalker nor glamorous courtesan; not a scheming, sultry siren. Just a faithful wife preparing to retire for the night.

And David? Probably thirty-nine years old, he was no sexually frustrated, night-walking peeping tom. Nor was he a sexually starved man on the prowl, like an animal in heat. At this time he already had more than seven wives and several concubines at his call. He had fathered seventeen children. So he was hardly looking for a new sexual conquest to evidence his virility. He had just what everyone else has had at times—

a sleepless night. I've had many. So have you. A night when thoughts seem to run and jump like wild goats all night, refusing to lie down. Perhaps he was thinking about his troops laying siege to the city of Rabbah. Or some other burden of state.

But it was still not late when David arose from his bed and went for a stroll on the roof of the palace—to think his problem through, to resolve his struggle with sleeplessness. Disinterestedly, he gazed in several directions, noting that the city was sleeping better than he was. Nearby, his eyes caught a small light through partially closed shutters. He glanced, once, twice—then gazed. A beautiful young woman taking her evening bath. Up to this point, everything is innocent and no one is to be blamed.

CONQUEST

Circumstances don't make a man, they reveal him. Like teabags, our real strength comes out when we get into hot water. There is nothing wrong with *happening* to see a beautiful woman bathing. Nothing wrong with recognizing her God-given physical attraction and charm. Nothing wrong with an involuntary rapid pulse beat, a surge of red-blooded manhood, an inner whisper, "Wow!" But now the struggle begins, the struggle with his fantasies, his flesh, his faith, and his future.

David knew well the law of God and His prohibition against adultery. He knew that according to the law a woman convicted of adultery could be stoned. As a young man he had memorized: "And thou shalt not covet thy neighbor's wife." And undoubtedly this was not his first such temptation. As a strong, ruddy young man in a king's palace, admired by the ladies of the realm, he had had his share of enticements and opportunities. But this was different—or was it? His thoughts raced in seesaw fashion. "More beautiful than any of my wives. So young, vibrant, appealing; she turns me on. I've been under a lot of pressure; I'm entitled to a little relaxation. I've kept God's laws for a long time; one slight infraction is not too serious. In fact, maybe God had me walk out here tonight so we could be together. Perhaps this is the purpose of a sleepless night, and just once . . . one act . . . not a long-term affair. It need not go beyond this night. And no one will ever know; I'll see to that." And to his servant, "Who is that girl? Whose house? I must know."

No hesitation, no waiting, weighing, considering consequences, turning away. He could not see beyond the moment; he was blinded by passion. A fuse begins to sparkle. He can see them in each other's embrace.

"She is Bathsheba, wife of Uriah," the servant reports.

David muses, "And Uriah is off to war. It all fits together so nicely. Uriah is a great soldier but he's probably not much of a husband or a lover—years older than she is—and he'll be away for a long time. This girl needs a little comfort in her loneliness. This is one way I can help her. No one will get hurt. I don't mean anything wrong by it. This is not lust—I've known that many times. This is love. This is not the same as finding a prostitute on the street. God knows that." And to the servant, "Bring her to me."

David evidently did not rationalize long. What he saw sparked his imagination and in less time than it takes to tell it, he was feeding a fantasy that had become an obsession. He had been drawn away by his own desires; these desires conceived, and he was pregnant with sin before Bathsheba ever got to his room and became pregnant with child.[6] Temptation appeals to desire, desire creates the fantasy, fantasy sparks the feeling, and the feelings cry out for the act.

THE COVER-UP

For days—probably several weeks—things went along as usual. Often David savored that memorable night, though he and Bathsheba were sworn to secrecy and had planned no further rendezvous. It was their private memory, locked in two hearts alone. Within a month or two, the signs—a missed menstrual period, morning sickness, dizziness, and the secret is exposed. "I'm pregnant."

From Adam's time and example, all men instinctively want to cover their tracks, "because their deeds are evil."[7] Watergate was nothing new. What was intended to be a clandestine and passing pleasure—an act—now requires a detailed strategy of deception—an attitude. Living a lie one night, if not confessed completely, requires many lies to cover it.

And the person with the reputation for integrity now resorts to every conceivable deception to save his own hide. Living a lie makes it easy to start telling lies, in fact necessitates it. "This is the first secret I've kept from my wife in eighteen years," an unfaithful husband confessed. "I feel like a heel having to make up so many lies when I've never done that before." The strategy is always the same. The tactics, timeworn: *protect yourself, blame others, eliminate the evidence*. Through all the centuries, man has come up with no new ways to hide.

Also, the well-taught Christian who chooses to conceal instead of confess tells the same deceptive stories as the philanderer who has never heard of the grace of God. A David—man after God's own heart—becomes cunning, treacherous, ruthless, and unconscionable.

In one master stroke of evil design, David moved quickly and decisively to do all three at once. Bring Uriah home from the war, let him sleep with Bathsheba a night or two, and send him back to the battle. Uriah would appreciate the R and R; he and everyone else would believe the baby was his, and David would be off the hook completely, free from exposure, blame, and responsibility. An ingenious scheme! The truth would be buried in Uriah's ignorance. And it would have worked out without a hitch if both Uriah and God had cooperated. David did not count on the integrity of his soldier or the displeasure of God.

Uriah came home at the king's order, reported on the battle, and was told to go home and relax for the night. Presents of food and wine were sent ahead to indicate David's delight in him and to set the stage for a merry evening. But this blood-and-guts soldier, though he may not have sensed any ulterior motive on David's part, could not bring himself to relax and enjoy his wife while his fellow officers were camped outside in a battle zone. He slept in the palace guardhouse.

With increasing determination and anger, David set him up for the next night. "If we get him drunk, we can get him down to the house and he'll want Bathsheba then. Even if he doesn't sleep with her, he'll be too drunk to remember what happened and that's just as good." But Uriah, though thoroughly drunk, slept another night with the guards.

Love and regard for this loyal soldier were turning to fear and resentment. "Then he must be removed from the scene. If it means I turn against those who have loved and served me, my friends are expendable. That's the way the ball sometimes bounces. I will sacrifice anyone—any relationship—to protect myself and keep the truth silent.

"Put Uriah at the front of the hottest part of the battle— and then pull back and leave him there to die."[8] He buried his sin in Uriah's grave. A continued extramarital affair always necessitates sacrifice. The selfish sacrifice of love, loyalty, relationships, respect, integrity, conscience—and the fellowship of God. "But the Lord was very displeased with what David had done."[9]

David's night of pleasure became a nightmare of pain. His baby died. His beautiful daughter, Tamar, was raped by half-brother Amnon. Amnon was killed by older brother Absalom. Absalom was separated from David for three years and came back to form a conspiracy against him. When Absalom was finally killed in an ambush, David broke into tears and sobbed, "Oh, Absalom, my son, my son."[10]

What changes a man chosen of God so that he becomes wily, sinister, a destroyer of all he and others hold dear? What turns a man's tender, responsive love for God into a hard, relentless determination to have his own way? The lessons from David are obvious and apply to all of us. Underscore them in your mind and heart.

1. No one, however chosen, blessed, and used of God, is immune to an extramarital affair.
2. Anyone, regardless of how many victories he has won, can fall disastrously.
3. The act of infidelity is the result of uncontrolled desires, thoughts, and fantasies.
4. Your body is your servant or it becomes your master.
5. A Christian who falls will excuse, rationalize, and conceal, the same as anyone else.
6. Sin can be enjoyable but it can never be successfully covered.
7. One night of passion can spark years of family pain.
8. Failure is neither fatal nor final.

These will all come into play in the following chapters.

CHAPTER 3

Why Do Partners Cheat?

The affair is a sign
of a need for help,
an attempt to compensate
for deficiencies
in the relationship
due to situational stress,
a warning that someone
is suffering.

Susan Squire

HINGS don't just happen. Every action has a cause. Actions do not arise spontaneously from a vacuum. There are contributing factors, pressuring forces, and personal reasons beneath the surface. Branches must have roots. And though the roots are seldom seen, they determine the size and character of the branches.

If a marriage is vibrant and growing, there are reasons. Growth is not automatic, imperceptible, and without cause. Relationships don't thrive if neglected or misused. And though the partners may not be able to articulate everything they're doing right, nevertheless, they are doing some things right.

Marriage failure is the same way. When a partner is involved in an affair—a one-night stand or a long-term relationship—there are reasons. Neither the guilty nor the innocent party may understand these reasons fully or describe them accurately. They may not know the deeper psychological, emotional, physical, and spiritual dimensions, and what may seem to be a valid reason for one may be an excuse for another.

The affair is a sign of a need for help—an attempt to compensate for deficiencies in the relationship, a warning that someone is suffering. Linda Wolfe summarizes, "Being unfaithful is a symptom, not a syndrome. Something is wrong in their marriage or their ability to be close to another human being in the same way that a fever is a manifestation of an infection. Extramarital affairs serve as an indicator of marriage malfunctioning."[1]

Causes of marital infidelity vary as much as the personalities involved, but I believe they can all be considered under one of three general headings: emotional immaturity, unresolved conflicts, or unmet needs.

EMOTIONAL IMMATURITY

Adolescence is usually feared by parents, as they fear the childhood diseases; they hope their children will get a light case and that there will not be any permanent scars. It is often a traumatic time with changing relationships, agonizing peer pressure, and questions about one's identity and future. This period was not intended to be permanent but is usually a bridge from the dependency of childhood to the interdependency of the adult. These transition years are often marked by immaturity, rebellion, fickleness, self-doubt, and experimentation. Unfortunately, some people in their forties or fifties are still adolescent in their behavior. Instead of marriage being our last best chance to grow up, according to Joseph Barth, it becomes a reflector of our perpetual immaturities.

Consider my friend Joe. Married three years—two children. During his dating years he liked to think of himself as God's gift to the girls and went from one partner to another. Ruggedly handsome, he had a cute smile and a confident manner which made him a charmer. Forced into marriage by his girl friend's unexpected pregnancy, he wanted to be faithful but still had a roving eye. According to him, his wife was all a wife could be—vivacious, sexually stimulating, unselfish, and, like him, a Christian. But in his mind he was still the unattached, flirtatious teen-ager. "I'm just not a one-woman man," he boasted with a twinkle in his eye.

By the time he and his wife came to me, he was eating business lunches at a go-go lounge, salivating over *Playboy* centerfolds, and visiting a girl on the side. He was vacillating between a wish for a strong marriage and his fluctuating adolescent appetites.

Self-doubt can set the stage for marital infidelity. I remember George well. He came from a family of high achievers—his father in top level management, his mother warm, outgoing, with many friends. His brothers and sisters were aggressive, confident, and all of them active in the church. As a boy he struggled with great expectations and comparisons, especially with his brothers, and secretly felt he wasn't as gifted, as likely to succeed. He had a poor self-esteem. He married Ann, a take-charge type, and they settled down to have a family.

Though he had everything that goes with success—good job, advancement opportunities, fine house—his inner conflict continued. "Everyone expects more of me; they don't accept me as I really am. Even in the bedroom, my wife responds, but reluctantly, as if to say, 'Do hurry and get this over with.' I'm really not the man I should be."

He felt castrated. He dreamed of a relationship where he wouldn't have this inner struggle—this always falling short—though adultery was totally contrary to all he believed and had been taught. Like most men, he wasn't looking for sex but for someone to prop up his sagging self-esteem.

The girl he met at the store was anything but the type he would have considered for a wife. Twice divorced, poor, unkempt—a tramp, but a champ at knowing how to build a man's ego. On his first visit to her place he was repulsed. It was the opposite of all he had known—little furniture, an old bed, a couple of folding chairs, a table, and one little throw rug. But it was an escape from everything that weighed down on him.

After their first sex together, he thought, "She likes me for myself, not for the person she tries to make of me. I am accepted. She enjoys me. I excite her." He was hooked. Like one touching a live wire, he couldn't let go. Later he said, "I never felt so much like a man as when I was with her."

Abigail Van Buren, the newspaper columnist who writes "Dear Abby," says, "A man picks up a tramp because he wants a female companion who is no better than he is. In her company he doesn't feel inferior. He rewards her by treating her like a lady. He treats his wife (who *is* a lady) like a tramp because he feels that by degrading her he will bring her down to his level. This makes him feel guilty. So in order to get even with his wife for making him feel guilty, he keeps right on punishing her."

Parental indulgence can prepare a child for perpetual immaturity and marriage infidelity. Permissive parents, fearful of thwarting their children's desires, give them everything they ever cry for. The children are never denied, but pampered, babied, and never taught the necessity or value of discipline. The adolescent who has everything, who has had every whim immediately indulged, will not become a marriage partner of strength and unselfishness. The man growing up without hearing and respecting the word NO will not take it as an answer when he is being tempted to satisfy his wants and desires.

Steve probably never understood that this was part of his problem. He'd come out of a strong Christian home where the Bible was honored, read, and followed. Going to church, special meetings, Bible camps, and a Christian college were all taken for granted and were characteristic of their family. The family's business interests flourished as did their standard of living. In every respect, they were a successful, exemplary Christian family. With one fatal flaw.

Whatever the children wanted, they could have. Whether toys or clothes, mopeds, snowmobiles, boats, cars, houses, travel—it made no difference, just say the word. The parents certainly meant no harm. "God has blessed us; let's enjoy it" was their attitude. Sacrifice, self-denial, discipline were familiar biblical terms but foreign to their vocabulary and lifestyle. When Steve married, it was love and luxury. Many years and problems later, when his marriage developed a fracture, he did the only thing he knew how to do: buy his wife more things. Bigger and better. He spent money like there was no tomorrow. But the rift widened. She wanted understanding, companionship, a solution. At this time a younger woman at the church sensed his frustration and discouragement and offered a warm smile, a warm hand, and ultimately, a warm body. Affairs were familiar ground for her and he was on her list.

Their affair plunged him into deep guilt as he struggled between denying his own desires and abandoning himself to them. Yet often he was strangely pleased with himself for giving in. His familiarity with the Bible only increased his guilt. When I reminded him that God's will prohibits this— "Do not commit adultery . . . do not covet thy neighbor's wife . . . if your hand offend you, cut it off"—he couldn't understand it. The essence of his response was, "How can you or anyone else tell me 'no.' I get what I want, always have, always will. I want this woman, regardless. Don't tell me what it will mean to break up my family, destroy her marriage, hurt the church testimony. This is what I want." Spoiled boy! His grieving parents never realized how they had contributed years ago to his failure and their present family disgrace.

Pride also sets up a man for a fall. As Solomon says in Proverbs, "Proud men end in shame, but the meek become wise." An emotionally mature person has a realistic sense of his own human weakness and the need for dependence upon God and other people. He does not parade his strength and flex his muscles before God and others.

A well-known evangelist became lifted up with pride. His work was prospering, radio and TV program thriving, invitations to speak increasing. He began to manipulate the people to his selfish ends. As he became more brazen, he traveled alone with his secretary. When a godly man asked him about this, he bragged, "I can handle it. Don't worry about me. And even if I decide to divorce my wife for this girl—no big deal.

People will forget all about it in a few months. It won't affect my ministry." Of course he fell—fell like a bird shot from the sky, and his marriage and ministry fell around him.

Another young man thought his ability at memorizing Scripture would make him secure. He had 2,000 verses under his belt but continued to have clandestine visits with a woman when her husband was away from home. "I shouldn't do it, but I think I'm strong." Pride blinded him. Knowledge alone is self-exalting. He might as well have memorized the dictionary. The Word in his mental grasp was not mixed with faith— the faith of action. He went like an ox to the slaughter, a moth to a flame.

Pride in one area of achievement may set us up to fall in another. ". . . lest being lifted up with pride he fall into the condemnation of the devil."[3] A best-selling Christian author, heady with the wine of recognition and prosperity, boldly engages in an adulterous relationship. The two areas are related. His fall is not in the area of his success; he is still writing. But his pride over his writing accomplishments led to his moral collapse.

"I was the most successful minister in town. Our church had grown by hundreds in a few months," one young pastor told me at a summer conference. "I was the talk of the community— recognized, praised, admired. No one had ever succeeded like this in the history of that church. Everyone was eating out of my hand. Then, for some crazy reason, I got involved with this girl and asked my wife for a divorce. Actually, our marriage was pretty good and I had no major complaints, but I couldn't give this girl up."

"Do you think your drift into this affair was in any way related to your success in the church?" I asked.

"Oh, absolutely," he agreed; "my egotism ruined me. I could do no wrong. I began to believe my own press releases. As the church continued to grow, I was lifted up with pride and this greased the slide for me on the moral front. Victory and defeat together. And of course, my relationship with the girl only fed my ego more. My wife wouldn't give me the divorce, so I was trapped."

Each person determines the extent of his own emotional immaturity. Affairs do not arise out of bad marriages, they are developed by immature people. A classic paragraph on maturity is Philippians 3:10-14:

Now I have given up everything else—I have found it to be the only way to really know Christ and to experience the mighty power that brought him back to life again, and to find out what it means to suffer and to die with him. So, whatever it takes, I will be the one who lives in the fresh newness of life of those who are alive from the dead.

I don't mean to say I am perfect. I haven't learned all I should even yet, but I keep working toward that day when I will finally be all that Christ saved me for and wants me to be.

No, dear brothers, I am still not all I should be but I am bringing all my energies to bear on this one thing: Forgetting the past and looking forward to what lies ahead, I strain to reach the end of the race and receive the prize for which God is calling us up to heaven because of what Christ Jesus did for us.

From this passage we learn that maturity has five elements:

Complete, irrevocable trust in Christ alone.
Recognition of my own human imperfections.
Commitment to lifelong learning and growth.
Keeping my future ahead of me, forgetting the past.
Anticipating, reaching, pressing for all God's good will for me.

All of these apply to marriage, too.

UNRESOLVED CONFLICTS

Conflicts in life are inevitable. In the intimacy and constant togetherness of marriage they are unavoidable. Children, money, sex, stress, in-laws—you name it. The young couple walking down the aisle with stars in their eyes, believing in a happily-ever-after, are in for a rude jolt. They are like the man who bought a record album for the song he wanted on the one side; when he got home he discovered it had another side with another song, totally different and less attractive.

Each person has his own set of idiosyncrasies brought over from childhood and experience. His habits are his own. He feels comfortable with them. Contemplating marriage, he's looking for someone who will also feel comfortable with him as he is and, at the same time, meet his emotional needs. This is usually someone quite different from himself, and that's part of the attraction. Now combine these two sets of temperaments, personalities, and individual characteristics, and there's bound to be disagreement and difficulty. Add to this the determined, selfish nature of each partner and you're bound to have more—fireworks!

In this kind of situation, for a marriage to survive and prosper, there must be negotiation, compromise, and acceptance. What has meaning for one person may have a different meaning or none at all for someone else. Some things mean little to us and we surrender them. Some of our partner's habits are innocent and we accept these and adjust. Other things are a source of constant irritation and we chafe and struggle with them. From our standpoint, they seem so unnecessary, unimportant, illogical, and impractical. We can't understand why our partner doesn't see the wisdom and advantage of our way, and want to change.

A stalemate develops. One partner insists on his way. The other matches with the same determination and continues to agitate. Communication on this point dies. Neither one has love strong enough to cover the other's weaknesses and focus on the other's strengths. This point of conflict then enters into the reason given for straying.

"The job is everything." The American man sees less of his family than any other husband and father in the world, noted Pearl Buck. The home wreckers are often the job, the corporation, the career. But no amount of business success can make up for failure at home. The extra promotion and larger paycheck hardly compensate for losing a loving spouse and alienating the children. Success isn't worth much to a businessman whose broken promises have ended in a broken home.

I still grieve over the young couple I met and counseled in Washington—Harold and Phyllis. They were both sharp, gifted, committed Christians, and had bright testimonies. I was impressed with their potential, so promising. God would use them greatly, I was sure. But the job—the work—the clients. He was a workaholic, pretty much his own boss. First one at the office, last one to leave. And, of course, it paid off handsomely. His salary, commissions, and promotions increased. Then came a new home, new car, new clothes, fine restaurants. Their one child, Brad, was growing up in good surroundings but with little father interest.

"You can't do everything you'd like to—there isn't time. And, of course, I've got to pay the bills, so I've got to keep hustling," Harold explained.

His responsibilities at work grew, and so did his son, but not his marriage. Phyllis began to feel increasingly left out, ignored. "Doesn't he realize we don't need more money, more things? We need *him.* The job is everything and I'm afraid of what it is going to mean to our boy. He and his father are growing farther apart and I can't keep making these lame excuses," she complained.

The boy joined Little League. Harold just couldn't squeeze

out time to see a practice, to attend the games. But he made arrangements: "Phyllis, be sure Brad has a way to the game and a ride back home." And when the son returned he couldn't even tell his father about their victory; he wasn't there. When he finally did get home, the boy was asleep. Every week, same story. Loneliness and resentment increased, driving mother and son to turn against the father.

"An affair with another man never entered my mind," Phyllis recounted. "This friendly guy was at all the games and took special note of Brad and me since we were always alone. One thing led to another, as they say."

Harold's wife became another man's mistress because Harold had a mistress: his job.

"Our whole life's a money struggle." "It was money that drove me into the arms of another man—at least, the conflict and pressure of money," complained Arlene.

Conflicts over money are customary in marriage. The income, expenses, credit, debts, coupled with the different meanings money has to each spouse, can make for a stressful, volatile situation. When a man loses his job and can't support his family, he often feels his masculinity is threatened. And in those circumstances, some men think that making a sexual conquest will help reconfirm their manhood.

But let's return to Arlene. "We had a chance to buy this house and it was a great bargain. But we had to furnish it, and just the basic things put us head over heels in debt. Then Bill had a car accident and there were a lot of things connected with it our insurance didn't cover. When I got pregnant we found that someone at Bill's office had neglected to include my name on the group insurance, so that wasn't covered either. I tried getting a job to help out, but by the time I'd paid the baby-sitter, bought clothes, and paid for my lunches and all that, I'd be making less than ten dollars a week. Our whole life is a money struggle. Every month it's a frantic shuffle to see what bills we can pay and what we'll have to put off. I get the nice job of calling creditors to tell them we can only pay half of what we owe this month. The constant worry, the embarrassment—you can just imagine what it's like.

"And then one day I ran into Dave, who was in my class in high school. He took me to lunch in a really fine, fancy restaurant. Oh, the relief! The sheer pleasure of getting to talk about ordinary, everyday things and not once hear him mention money. The guilt I feel about my affair is like little drops of acid eating away at the back of my mind. But I have to have some escape, some release from this constant financial worry and tension."

"My mother-in-law isn't bossy—she's tyrannical." Do the in-laws encourage marital infidelity? Most of them are very anxious that their offspring do well and be a credit to the family name. And having the grandparents nearby and available is important to children to give them a sense of history and continuity.

But Joanne learned the hard way that the health of one's own marriage must take precedence over any negative influence and intrusion of the relatives, whoever they are.

She didn't take action soon enough. She was only twenty-five and worked part-time as a licensed practical nurse. Her reaction to the end of her affair, as well as the reason for it, was fairly characteristic.

"Jim's a darling—somewhat passive, but I love him very much. If anyone had ever told me I'd cheat on him I'd have laughed in that person's face. But I did.

"It started when my mother-in-law broke her ankle and came to stay with us while it healed. My mother-in-law isn't bossy; she's tyrannical. She wants this, this, and this done right now and done her way. Supposedly she was going to stay a few weeks, but she moved in bag and baggage and within a week she had our house and our lives arranged to her satisfaction. It was evident to me that she planned to stay for good.

"I didn't feel like I should say anything; after all, she was Jim's mother. But I got more and more resentful. I started spending as much time as possible away from home, and one day Fred, the son of one of my patients, offered to drive me home and suggested we stop for a cup of coffee on the way.

"That's how it started. It lasted three months. One day Fred said something about being grateful to my mother-in-law for making me want to spend so much time with him. That started me thinking and I realized several things. I didn't love Fred. Really, I was using him in a crazy way to hit back at my mother-in-law and at Jim for not standing up to her. I had never told Jim how I felt; I just expected him to know and I got angry when he didn't.

"I broke off with Fred, then told Jim his mother had to go. He was surprised and, I think, relieved, because he found her an apartment—on the other side of town—the next day. I'm ten times happier now."

"We disagreed about our daughter." "What do you see as the basic problem in your marriage that would relate in any way to your present infidelity? Your marriage always seemed strong and you and your wife compatible." This was my question to a businessman in California when he asked for help in extricating himself from his extramarital affair.

"My wife and I had a serious disagreement over one of our children," he answered immediately. "It became a wall between us."

"Tell me how it developed to this point," I suggested.

"Our daughter was beginning to date and neither one of us really knew what to do. My wife was fearful that she would come home pregnant very soon, considering some of the crowd she was running with. So she said, 'Forbid her to go out with them. We must protect her; it's for her own good.' I was concerned too, but wanted to approach it differently. I wanted to tell her we trusted her and put her on her honor. We discussed the merits of each approach until there was no more to say. But we kept on talking. Not talking really, anymore. We were arguing, criticizing, lashing out.

"Naturally, our daughter played this to the hilt. She knew that if we were fighting each other she'd be off the hook. She sided with me and against her mother. Feeling rejected, my wife accused me of being weak and vacillating—and maybe I was. The blow came, as far as I'm concerned, when she said she had lost all respect for me. I was devastated. The problem had shifted from the girl to our marriage. Attacks became more vicious and dredged up other things that had long since been forgotten. All of our dreams were collapsing.

"I walked about like a zombie. What had been a great marriage seemed now to be a hollow shell. I wasn't looking for an affair—I've always been faithful—but I was looking for a little comfort, a boost, a prop for my sagging spirit, I guess. This other woman provided that."

"An audience with a queen." "Nobody could understand it when I found somebody else and moved out," Frank said, "—not even Helen, although I tried to talk it over with her. It was her crazy attitude about sex that did it. For Helen even to think of lovemaking, everything had to be just right. The house had to be cleaned, the ironing done, her hair looking good, etc., etc., and she had to be perfectly happy with me in every way. If there had been any kind of a problem in the last week, that was it. I was walking a tight-rope. And I had to let her know in plenty of time that I was in the mood. If I didn't, she'd pretend to be asleep or say she had a headache. I had eight years of feeling like I was trying to schedule an audience with a queen. Every time I felt loving was just too much. It's a shame. It's a shame because in a lot of ways she's a very good wife."

"A terrible housekeeper." Sam's complaint was the opposite. "Lucy was a terrible housekeeper—just never got around to ironing my shirts, and spent hours on the phone, usually talking about our private life. So when I would get irritated or even just try to talk to her about it, she'd grab my arm and head for the bedroom. She thought all of our problems could be solved in bed, without her making any other effort at all to change her ways. I had to get some relief. The first time I met this divorcée at her place, it was clean, neat, attractive. Anybody would feel at home. It was comfortable and relaxing. The sex was nothing special, but the apartment was just such a pleasant place to be."

"A conservative background." In observing thirty-three-year-old Mary across my desk, I was impressed with her plainness. Hair, lack of make-up, dress, all said she must have had a conservative religious background. She fidgeted hesitantly but finally sobbed out her story.

"I can't believe Tom would ever do this, but I found this note from Diane in his pocket. He's always been active in church, but is very quiet and not the aggressive type. And Diane—we're in the same golf league, live only three blocks apart, and our paths cross constantly."

When Tom came to me a few days later, he was just what she'd said—clean-cut, reserved, congenial. During his account of the affair he quietly noted, "My wife is so frugal and plain. Her family was this way. She dresses in such out-of-style clothes that she stands out in a crowd. I'm embarrassed, though I want to be proud of her. Over and over I've told her to get something better, but she refuses. A little stubborn, I think."

"Give me an example," I asked.

"Well, just recently I asked her to get a dress that wasn't dragging around her ankles, but she thought I wanted her to dress immodestly and she wouldn't do it. Even in our golf league, the other men's wives look so much sharper. Mary could look great if she could rid herself of these rigid notions. This is really the big point of our disagreement and conflict."

"Super-clean Jean." Conflicts stemming from different standards of cleanliness are not only common, but also the source of ongoing arguments that gradually erode the partners' feelings for each other. Each person in his subconscious mind has an idealized version of what "home" should be like, based on early childhood experience. When these differences exist, the resulting marital problem is far more important than any disagreement over sex and money.

Jean was a perfectionist—and Lysol-clean. Bob groaned, "She's the type of wife who, if I got up in the middle of the night for a drink of water, would make the bed. Literally, she will not let the family use the living room, for fear they'll mess it up." She was as fastidious about her body as about her house, and would demand that her husband withdraw before ejaculating because she didn't want his semen inside her.

"The sound just wore me out." What is more common than the self-righteous mate whose nagging and criticism drive her partner right out of her life?

"My wife nags the way most people breathe—without realizing it." And Harvey's comments about his wife were not all negative. "She's always looked good, was a good mother, good cook, and good housekeeper. But man, the slightest little thing and off she'd go. I got so I'd rather sit in the car in the garage than go into the house at night.

"One night we were driving home and I didn't change into a turn lane soon enough. Eight blocks later she was still harping on it. The sound beating against my ears just wore me out. You get to where you don't hear words, just a continual stream of noise. Finally, I just had to get out completely and find other quiet female company. And believe me, that company is not hard to find."

"Nagging about [mistakes]," says Solomon, "parts the best of friends. It is better to live in a corner of an attic than in a beautiful home with a cranky, quarrelsome woman. The constant dripping on a rainy day and a cranky woman are much alike. You can no more stop her complaints than you can stop the wind or hold onto anything with oil-slick hands."[4] These verses would apply to nagging husbands, too.

Disagreement doesn't hurt a marriage, but criticism kills it. We can strongly disagree on many matters, respect each other's views, work it through, and still love each other. But when the disagreement turns to criticism of the other person, no one can take that very long. Attacking the person instead of working on the problem is a sure way to suggest to your partner that he/she might have made a mistake in marrying you. And he might look elsewhere to remedy that mistake.

"Maybe it's just the mid-life blues." Steve, head of the company that was working on my lawn this past week, was bluntly candid as I asked him about his marriage. "Sure, I'm married, but it's 'Dullsville.' The whole thing's a grave. Gone from fair to worse. My wife doesn't seem to understand some of my struggles right now—*I* don't even understand them. But I've worked my tail off—made it good—and what has it gotten me? We're just getting old. Maybe I've got what they call the mid-life blues. But half of my life is behind me, the kids are gone—a man is entitled to have a little fun."

So his affair—more than one, in his case—related to his mid-life age and stage in life and confirmed the study by Doctors Blood and Wolfe which revealed that only half of middle-aged married couples are in any way satisfied with their marriages. Some couples stay together until the children are reared, and then split. Most don't wait, however. Today 45 percent of all children will live in a single-parent home before they reach eighteen.

Marital satisfaction often takes a nose dive after children arrive. The routine becomes a rut and the marriage gets tired, flat, and monotonous. As the partners grow older, they grow apart and experience an emotional divorce. There is a gradual erosion of their mutual hopes and dreams and the only thing they share anymore is the bathroom.

And change is difficult—costly. It becomes more difficult to renew and renegotiate an old marital contract than to make a new one with someone else.

Steve concluded, "I know I'm giving my wife the shaft but I'm not an old has-been, and I'm not about to shrivel up with an old lady when there are some young things out there who think I've still got something to offer. I don't intend to miss the last train out of town."

UNMET NEEDS

"My partner doesn't understand or meet my needs." Every husband and wife has felt this at some time though they may never have verbalized it audibly. When needs are not met, the door is opened for infidelity—someone else to meet those needs. Well-known family counselor Dr. James Dobson says it succinctly:

Great needs arise. The greater the needs for pleasure, romanticism, sex, and ego satisfaction, the greater the needs within marriage and the louder these voices scream. A need accumulates and is not being met. And the person is usually crying to others around them, "Meet my needs. Hear me. Love me. Understand me. Care for me." And these cries are not heard, understood, or responded to. We're at home, we're living together, but we're not meeting each other's needs. And the needs get louder; and when the needs get greater then the voices calling people into infidelity get greater.[5]

Marriage is a need-meeting relationship. It was so during the courtship and continues till the last day a couple is together. No one is so unselfish or altruistic that he marries with a pure desire to meet someone else's need and ask nothing for himself. And wanting our needs to be met is neither selfish nor sinful. It has been said that love is the accurate estimate and supply of another's needs.

Adam and Eve, though perfect and innocent, had various kinds of needs. God created them that way. They had social, emotional, physical, and spiritual needs—and this was before their fall into sin. In fact, their fall was actually the attempt to satisfy these needs in a way and at a time contrary to the plan of the Creator.

God put man with his needs in a position where his needs could be met.

1. He was placed in a beautiful garden and was told to cultivate it, keep it, and eat from it. *His needs for beauty, work, food could be satisfied from his surroundings.*
2. He was not left alone but was given another person and told to share, unite, procreate. *His needs for companionship, intimacy, continuity, and family would be met through other people.*
3. He was given fellowship with God. *His needs for ultimate meaning, purpose, and eternal life would be met by God alone.*

Only certain needs can be met in marriage, by another person. Not all. But the essence of the marriage promise is "I will meet these needs." The wedding vows say it:

"To have and to hold"—commitment
"For better or for worse"—belonging
"For richer, for poorer"—loyalty
"In sickness and in health"—support
"To love and to cherish"—faithfulness
"Till death do us part"—companionship

That is a tall order. No wonder we all sometimes fail. I'm not suggesting we dilute the vows but rather that we understand how they're translated and applied to our partner's everyday needs.

The needs of two people seldom dovetail perfectly, but when each partner is seriously seeking to meet the needs of the other, the problem of the third party has little opportunity to develop.

We have five basic needs that a marriage partner can meet.

ATTENTION

"Did you ever hear of the great stone face?" a woman asked her friend.

"Yes, I think I have," the friend replied.

"I married him," the woman stated. "He doesn't listen and he doesn't talk."

Sara wrote me after our counseling sessions, "It's going to be hard for me to give up the love I had for someone else and to say no to the first person who really listened to me. For thirteen years with Bruce I had felt so unloved and unwanted. He never notices my cooking, the way I look, how I try to keep the house for him. He never pays attention to me. He takes me for granted and I really don't think I'm important to him."

One guilty straying husband said, "I'd come to feel like no more than a piece of furniture. I was nobody around my own home, nobody worth noticing, listening to, or loving. I got fed up. Not long ago I walked right out the door. This is what I mean," he said. "I came home one night some weeks ago and my wife was putting the baby to bed. I started to kiss her but she turned up her cheek and talked about the baby's rash. Did you ever try to kiss someone with a safety pin in her mouth? Why couldn't she look at me? Talk to me? Do I have to break out in a diaper rash or spit up my food to get her to notice me? I'm the guy she married. I'd have to break a leg or come down with pneumonia to get her to notice that I'm around."[6]

ACCEPTANCE

Every person has a deep-seated need to be accepted for his or her own individual value. It is our job to love our partners, God's job to change them. Author John Drescher quotes counselor Ira J. Tanner, "Any attempt to move one's mate in an effort to match them to our fantasies is arrogance on our part and an insult to them. It divides, breeds anger, and causes even greater loneliness."[7] And, I might add, it pushes the mate into other, more accepting, arms.

Ruth and Jack were personal friends of Evelyn's and mine—in fact, neighbors. But her affair brought them to me for counsel. Jack was ambitious, hard-driving, demanding, an aggressive witness for Christ—a button-holer. Ruth was fairly quiet—attractive in appearance, outgoing, and congenial. A winsome witness.

Jack's own inflexible Christian standards drew some people but repelled others. They were applied to one and all, in the church and out, producing in some false guilt, in others only pity—for Jack. Every member in the family felt the pressure. Some rebelled; some knuckled under.

Ruth said, "I love the Lord very much but I just couldn't please my husband. I wasn't growing spiritually as fast as he thought I should. He was always checking to see how much I read my Bible. My body just ran down so I couldn't keep going to church meetings every night of the week. I just had to stay home. Jack interpreted this as backsliding and criticized me in front of the children till our whole family was bickering constantly. He then blamed me for the trouble in our family because I was 'drifting away from the Lord.' He wanted me to be Mother Theresa, Betty Crocker, and Cheryl Ladd rolled into one. He was determined to squeeze me into his mold. Nothing I could do pleased him anymore.

"Sin—adultery—was the farthest thing from my mind since the day I became a Christian. I wasn't looking for sex— even that had deteriorated in our marriage, too. I wasn't even looking for an affair to get revenge, make my husband pay, or even get his attention. I was just beat. That was all. And when the neighbor down the street noticed me, smiled a few times, talked pleasantly, and liked me the way I was—that was it. I was a dead pigeon."

AFFECTION

Many partners cheat in marriage for nothing more at the start than a desire for a little affection. The things that put the glow in the days of courtship and early marriage—touching, holding, hugging, kissing—cannot be stashed away now in the closet with all the old wedding announcements.

"We're married now; we're not kids anymore." He thinks, "Why do you have to keep chasing the streetcar once you've caught it?" She feels, "Once you catch the fish, you can throw away the bait."

"We haven't touched each other for over two years. Almost literally. Certainly we've had no sex relations, but we actually hardly ever touch, at least not intentionally." These were the words of a pastor's wife who had come to one of our seminars. She was about fifty, a little stocky, hair pulled back, rather plainly dressed, and she looked like a highly organized administrative type. Her voice beginning to crack, she continued, "I've not been much of an affectionate type, not that I don't enjoy it, but my husband and I've had to work so hard to keep our churches going. For twenty-three years we've pastored, mostly smaller churches. You know how it is; you do all the work—teach, sing, organize, visit, janitor. Always overloaded, always exhausted.

"When my husband evidenced no desire to show affection or any need for it, I assumed he was just that kind and those things didn't interest him—weren't necessary. So I didn't push it either, and kind of stayed out of his way. I was never taught that these things are important to a man."

"How did your husband get involved with this other woman?" I ventured.

"Well, she offered to do some volunteer work in the church office. We didn't know her too well but we needed the help. We wondered, a time or two, if we should keep her, since she dressed in such an obviously sensual way. But my husband felt that since she was a new Christian he could help her. I felt she'd be no temptation to him since he was not interested in affection." By now she was sobbing.

"Then what happened?"

"How blind I was, oh, how blind! How mistaken I was. She would make a special point to be in his office for every little excuse. She kidded him, touched him playfully, and, well, something came alive in him, I guess. He became a different man. That's when he told me he didn't love me anymore and was going to leave the ministry and move in with her. It was unbelievable."

Many women are affection starved, too. Author Evelyn Miller Berger recalls the familiar, yet humorous, story I first heard years ago. A couple driving along a lonely road one night were held up and told to hand over their money. "But I don't have any money," protested the man driving the car. The bandit ordered him out of the car to be searched. Sure enough, the man had no money. Then the wife was ordered out of the car. When she was searched, she was found to have no money either, and was told to get back in the car. As she did, she said, "If you'll frisk me again, I'll write you a check."

ADMIRATION

Mark Twain said, "I can live for two months on a good compliment." For every negative comment a parent makes to a child, he must give four positive comments to keep a balance. So in marriage. Verbal praise nourishes the relationship. According to my friend Dr. Ed Wheat, "A wife's sense of her own beauty depends greatly on what her husband thinks of her. She must be nourished emotionally with praise and never diminished by criticism."[8]

Famous author Marabel Morgan asks, "What motivates the man to be responsible and to succeed in his ambitions? What one incentive will help a man remain stable, faithful and loving to his wife and family? Admiration can put back the skip in a husband's walk, a sparkle in his eyes and the flutter in his heart. He will dare to dream again and believe in his abilities because you've told him you do."[9]

What traits should we admire? *"Concentrate on his virtues,"* say Lou Beardsley and Toni Spry. *"His role as a husband and father.*

His appearance and manner of dress.
His mental capacities.

His dependability on the job.
His masculine strength.
His love for the Lord.
His athletic ability and coordination.
His sense of humor.
His courage.
His tenderness and sexual capacities.
These are just a start."[10]

A husband should read Proverbs 31 and the Song of Solomon. Underline every quality, ability, and area of beauty mentioned about those two wives. Apply them all to your own wife and make your own admiration list.

ACTIVITIES

Many marriages crash on the rocks of infidelity because they become dull. Boredom sets in. The routine becomes a rut. Go to work, come home, watch TV, go to bed—week after monotonous week.

"We don't do anything together anymore," is a common wifely complaint. "No dates together without the kids, no recreation, no concerts, no shared interests or projects, no fun."

"My husband and I used to go out without the children three or four times a week, which was too much. But then we stopped and didn't go any place, which was just as bad."

This woman's husband, just recovering from his affair with a girl in his office, agreed. "I felt we needed to spend more time together—just the two of us—doing things like hobbies, projects, etc."

Great or potentially great marriages all suffer if neglected. Read again Benjamin Franklin's familiar verse: "A little neglect may breed great mischief; for want of a nail the shoe was lost; for want of a shoe the horse was lost; for want of a horse the rider was lost, being overtaken and slain by an enemy—all for want of a little care about a horseshoe nail."

No one person can meet all of another person's needs. Some needs are met by others, some by our vocations, some by God alone. To expect one's partner to provide what only God can provide is certain disappointment. No one can take His place. And the peace, contentment, and strength He provides will affect every other area of our marriage relationship.

But just as no person can take God's place, God does not take the partner's place. We have been created to fill needs for each other that only another person can fill. A moving poem by famous poet Ella Wheeler Wilcox, though written nearly one hundred years ago, graphically tells the modern story.[11]

AN UNFAITHFUL WIFE TO HER HUSBAND

Branded and blackened by my own misdeeds
I stand before you; not as one who pleads
For mercy or forgiveness, but as one,
After a wrong is done,
Who seeks the why and wherefore.

Go with me,

Back to those early years of love, and see
Just where our paths diverged. You must recall
Your wild pursuit of me, outstripping all
Competitors and rivals, till at last
You bound me sure and fast
With vow and ring.
I was the central thing
In all the Universe for you just then.
Just then for me, there were no other men.
I cared

Only for tasks and pleasures that you shared.
Such happy, happy days. You wearied first.
I will not say you wearied, but a thirst
For conquest and achievement in man's realm
Left love's barque with no pilot at the helm.
The money madness, and the keen desire
To outstrip others, set your heart on fire.
Into the growing conflagration went
Romance and sentiment.
Abroad you were a man of parts and power—
Your double dower
Of brawn and brains gave you a leader's place;
At home you were dull, tired, and commonplace.
You housed me, fed me, clothed me; you were kind;
But oh, so blind, so blind.
You could not, would not, see my woman's need
Of small attentions; and you gave no heed
When I complained of loneliness; you said
"A man must think about his daily bread
And not waste time in empty social life—
He leaves that sort of duty to his wife
And pays her bills, and lets her have her way,
And feels she should be satisfied."

Each day.

Our lives that had been one life at the start,
Farther and farther seemed to drift apart.
Dead was the old romance of man and maid.
Your talk was all of politics or trade.
Your work, your club, the mad pursuit of gold
Absorbed your thoughts. Your duty kiss fell cold
Upon my lips. Life lost its zest, its thrill,

Until

One fateful day when earth seemed very dull
It suddenly grew bright and beautiful.

Why Do Partners Cheat?

I spoke a little, and he listened much;
There was attention in his eyes, and such
A note of comradeship in his low tone,
I felt no more alone.
There was a kindly interest in his air;
He spoke about the way I dressed my hair.
And praised the gown I wore.
It seemed a thousand, thousand years and more
Since I had been so noticed. Had mine ear
Been used to compliments year after year,
If I had heard you speak
As this man spoke, I had not been so weak.
The innocent beginning
Of all my sinning
Was just the woman's craving to be brought
Into the inner shrine of some man's thought.
You held me there, as sweetheart and as bride;
And then as wife, you left me far outside.
So far, so far, you could not hear me call;
You might, you should, have saved me from my fall.
I was not bad, just lonely, that was all.

A man should offer something to replace
The sweet adventure of the lover's chase
Which ends with marriage. Love's neglected laws
Pave pathways for the "Statutory Cause."

CHAPTER 4

Marriage Myths and Legends

*When anyone expects
something out of marriage
it was never intended to deliver,
he is doomed to feeling
disappointed, disillusioned,
and angry.
This can become an excuse
for an affair
or an opportunity
to grow up.*

OST of the things that most of us believed when we entered marriage are not true. These myths and legends have been passed through many generations, and though everyone's experience denies them, we still hold to them as tenaciously as a drowning man to an unconnected rope. I've talked with second- and third-time divorcées who still believe and hope these myths will prove true for them the next time around.

Believing these legends creates conscious and unconscious expectations in people that doom their marriage from the start and set it up for infidelity. They become disappointed, weakened, and vulnerable.

Belief determines behavior. You can't believe wrong and come out right. You can't think sickness and come up with health, cultivate failure but find success, believe in fables and enjoy reality.

Sad to say, some of these myths are perpetuated in the church, the Bible class, the seminar. I have no desire to upset anyone's faith. On the contrary, I want that faith to be honest, realistic, and truly biblical. But Christians sometimes believe more than is in the Bible because of a proof-text method of interpretation or a juvenile hope that God will assume the responsibilities for them.

We all want packaged answers, assembly line solutions. We want an authoritarian teacher to tell us what to think, not how to think. To assure us that "this belief," "this plan," "this method," "this approach" is *the* answer to all problems and is the only Bible truth. And, of course, we think that these teachers alone have these truths.

Let's consider four of these dangerous myths.

MYTH NUMBER ONE: "MADE IN HEAVEN"

This trademark on any marriage means what the expensive manufacturer's label means on a pair of jeans: quality. No flaws, no rips, the finest material, hand stitching, designer styling. As one company says, the quality goes in before the name goes on.

So if our marriage is made in heaven, if God brings us together, it is bound to prosper. That didn't work in the first marriage and it hasn't worked since. No one would question that God brought Adam and Eve together, but that didn't assure family success.

The unspoken suppositions of this myth go like this: "Since heaven is a perfect place, any plan coming out of there brings with it its own success. There is only one right man or one right woman—the one person in the world I can be happy with—with whom I really am compatible. And God has settled it that we will get together somehow. And furthermore, if God chooses my partner for me and brings us together, we will surely not have the problems and difficulties other couples have. Little or no adjustment will be necessary. We are made for each other."

Let's put all of these daydreams back in the fairy-tale books with the white knight and the princess, where they belong.

One fallacy of this myth is predestination. If God predestined us for this relationship and if it doesn't work out, it's His fault. We are only passive participants in the game. God plans it, makes the rules, and assures its prosperity. When unforeseen difficulties come, with Adam we blame God, "the partner *You* gave me," we give up our faith, or we deny the reality of the problem.

Also, *believing this legend gives false comfort and security.* "God made us for each other" implies that our personalities dovetail—our temperaments are complementary. We are ill-prepared for the shocks of disagreement and conflict, times when everything hits the fan—the stalemate—the impasse—the blowout.

Third, *this myth becomes an excuse.* When romantic love fades, its flame flickers. The old snap is gone, your partner doesn't perform the same, and deterioration sets in. Then comes the cop-out: "I guess God didn't really bring us together in the first place. Maybe our marriage was only secular and God wasn't really in it. He really didn't bind us together, so we better separate." One woman who told me this added, "And we finally found a Scripture that tells us we can get a divorce." That sounds spiritual but it is as phony as a fish wearing glasses.

I've heard this scores of times, and I always answer: "I do not know whether or not your marriage was made in heaven but I do know that all the maintenance work is done on earth."

A word about this "right man—right woman" theory. It is hard for me to believe that God would so limit one's possibilities for happiness. Death, accident, or chance separation could prevent the marriage of one particular man to one particular woman. I think it would be possible to build a great marriage with any one of a number of people of the other sex. If two people understand the active nature of love and are committed to the well-being of each other, they can find marital satisfaction.

In many nonwestern cultures there is no acquaintance or love before marriage. Marriages are arranged by parents. An individual has no say in who his or her partner will be, and certainly the partners do not know or love each other. Yet many strong and beautiful marriages have come out of this kind of arrangement. Most real love is developed after marriage and requires the same kind of effort in whatever culture.

This myth also immobilizes. Sincere Christian young people wait in apprehension for some guiding star—some dramatic direction written in a cloud: M T P N—Marry This Person Now! One young man, obviously sincere and troubled, almost begged me, "Please tell me if I should marry this girl. We're both committed to Christ and we believe we love each other. We've been going together a long time and it seems to be the right thing but I haven't had any clear signal yet. No assurance that everything will work out—no distinct guidance."

Now, let's not be accused of leaving God out of this marriage picture. Here are the facts. God does have a plan for every person's life, and He will guide us into that plan if we want it. And that plan certainly includes two basic directions: the work we are to do and our marriage—our place and our partner, if marriage is His will for us.

If a couple is really committed to doing God's will and patiently seeks it through His Word, prayer, and counsel with mature Christians, God will bring the right people together. While Adam fell asleep in the will of God, God made him a wife and brought her to him.

Abraham's servant was sent to Iraq to find a wife for Isaac. The servant wanted God's will and prayed, "Show me the right girl, the one who is generous, the one who offers to serve, to go the second mile."[1] God likes to answer that kind of prayer.

Consider my case. Evelyn was a vivacious, gifted, generous, and popular girl when we first met. She had been engaged twice before to Christian men and had no lack of admiring suitors. My first reaction upon recovering from the delightful shock of getting acquainted was, "I must rescue this girl from all her admirers." We became engaged—not that same day, of course, but not many months later. We both really wanted God's will in our lives and felt that He had brought us together.

After a six-month engagement, we disagreed on whether to get married then or to go on to further schooling. We broke up completely. With finality. I went on to school. She returned to her home five hundred miles away. We maintained no contact and destroyed or returned all the mementos of our relationship, the letters, the pictures, rings, etc. And though we were totally out of each other's lives and greatly separated, I would often remember what a great girl she was and unconsciously compare my present dates to her. Evelyn still felt deep in her heart that God had brought us together originally, even though everything now indicated we would never see that happen.

Many months passed. Evelyn, coming to the conclusion that our friendship was totally gone, reluctantly made other plans. She took another job and her whole life headed in a different direction. Ultimately she met a fine Christian man and was engaged again and planned for their wedding. I had some reason to send her a note at this time, not knowing of her impending marriage to this good man—and, of course, not knowing that the invitations had been sent out, the showers given, the bridesmaids' dresses made, the minister engaged, and all the other preparations completed.

My note kindled an old flame. Her response awakened my appreciation of her. I made a telephone call. Her sparkling spirit captivated me again. The wedding was called off five days ahead of time and we picked up where we had left off. And there have been many side benefits. I still eat toast every morning from the toaster someone gave her for the other man!

Now I'm not suggesting this as a pattern. It was a pretty

close call. But we both know and have never had a doubt that God brought us together to build a strong marriage and to help other marriages.

MYTH NUMBER TWO: "FIND MY ROLE"

As far back as I can remember, every sermon I heard on the home stressed two or three points. There were always these two: "The husband is the boss; the wife is in subjection." If the third point was included, it was "Make those kids mind, and have a family altar." Since those impressionable years I've seen many couples with their roles clearly defined but their marriage on the skids—homes where they read Ezekiel at the family altar and the kids couldn't wait to break away.

I question whether the scene has changed much, though certainly there are more good family life resources than at any time in church history. The practical and biblical insights on marriage and parenting available today are wonderful. But the unbalanced teaching on roles continues as if identifying and assuming your unique role assures marriage success. Ministers and seminar leaders, both men and women, are still laying heavy guilt trips on women about their proper role, but I don't hear much about husbands "loving their wives as Christ loved the church," and about what that means. In my own early ministry, I could speak for hours on the woman's responsibility but I could muster only a sentence or two for the men, and that just before the benediction.

In one of our seminars together, Dr. Howard Hendricks said many Christian men are like frustrated sergeants hitting their wives over the head with the Bible and repeating the one verse they've memorized, "Submit, submit; find your place and stay there."

Other discouraged Christian wives are sighing, "If only my

husband would take his proper role as head of this house our problems would be solved."

Granted, each partner in marriage has a special function, though our purpose is not to dissect that here. God created us with male and female characteristics, unique gifts, and spiritual responsibilities. We are equal in value and importance, but different in function. No one is left to choose the place he will fill and how he will fill it. There is design and order.

However, just assuming a role and taking authority is not the same as biblical leadership. I can take that position and still be self-centered, bossy, and tyrannical. And when my attitude is wrong, my relationships wither.

I was the leader in our family. There was no question about that. But I didn't understand Jesus' prescription that a leader is the servant of all: giving, ministering, redeeming.[2] I could give orders but I couldn't serve. I was decisive but stern, unyielding. I was a good provider but provided little reinforcement for my wife's gifts. In my view, Ephesians 5:20-33 was written primarily for the wife.

. . . Until the pinch came. Strains in our marriage took me back to that passage again and I was devastated. Words that I hadn't really seen before jumped off the page: *submitting yourself . . . love . . . gave himself . . . sanctify and cleanse his bride . . . present her without blemish . . . love wife as own body . . . nourish . . . cherish . . . members . . . leave/cleave . . . joined . . . one flesh . . . love as himself . . . as Christ loved the church.*

How did Christ love the church? Whatever He asked of His people, He did first. He commands us to love; He did it first. We must forgive; He forgave first. We are called to carry the cross; He carried it first. We must sacrifice; He did it first.

So man is the initiator. He forgives first, sacrifices, forgives, reinforces, accepts first. He models something for his wife as

Christ did for the church. That is more than wearing a title or being a divine patrolman. This takes away his sense of superiority and he realizes he cannot do this without the strength of God.

MYTH NUMBER THREE:
"MARRIAGE WILL MAKE ME HAPPY"

One reason marriage gets a bad press these days is that it isn't the cure-all that it is supposed to be. And no people in the world make greater demands on marriage than Americans. It does not do what parents, friends, education, and success have also been unable to do—make us happy. We still believe marriage is our great hope. It will separate us from our past, give us all the love we need now, and assure us of a contented old age. "Happily ever after" is still in our dreams.

The wedding ceremony is an open admission to the world that we believe we have found someone who will make us happy. One divorced husband told a minister friend what many would not have the courage to say, "God bless my dear wife; she tried so hard. I gave that woman three of the best years of my life, hoping she could learn to understand me and make me feel like a man. She just didn't have it in her. She simply did not know how to make me happy."

His parents had tried and failed. Others failed. So he took a wife and gave her a shot at it. And she failed. But he'll try again, I'm sure, and give someone else the privilege. And she will also fail. Every new march down the aisle for this overgrown boy is doomed to increase his disappointment and misery. He's a dreamer.

One man wondered aloud to me why his marriages didn't last. He's already been through number five. He's an angry man and his explosions destroy all he really wants. But the wife is always to blame. She didn't produce happiness.

Three fallacies make up this myth:

Marriage will compensate for past failures. "My mother didn't like me; my dad didn't button my pants right once; we lived on the wrong side of town; my schoolteacher failed me. Marriage will be a haven where I can drop anchor—I will be accepted. All the past will be forgotten. It will be a new beginning." It will be a new relationship all right, but the past will trail you like a bloodhound. We marry for all the wrong reasons—to get away from a bad home, to get even, to prove something. Problems in marriage will bring back the past, and the past will determine how we deal with these problems. Your past will affect your marriage more than your marriage will alter your past.

Marriage doesn't change the past; it reveals it. Even God can't change the past; it has happened, it is fixed. But God can free us from its tyranny. Then we can learn from the past and use it as a platform from which to launch positive counteractions.

The second fallacy: *My partner will provide what I need.* If I believe this, I create a controlled dependency. I become an emotional cripple. The quality of my life is determined by others. I am not my own person. They act, I react. They put on the show, I am a spectator. I'm the leaner; when they move, I fall. They catch a cold, I'm the one who sneezes. I live through them and make them morally obligated to provide my well-being. When they fail to produce what I think I need, they are blamed for my failure. I have given them the power to destroy me.

A young minister's wife sobbed out her confession to David Wilkerson: "There's absolutely no hope for our marriage now. We're in two different worlds. He is so wrapped up in his work; he has no time for me and the children. My whole world has been wrapped up in him, but now I'm getting tired of staying home waiting for him. I'm not accomplishing anything on my own. I don't even know if I love him anymore."

David wisely answered, "What a shame that all your happiness depends only on what your husband does. If he is a good husband, if he treats you the way you think you should be treated, if he spends a little time with you—then you may find a little happiness. But when he lets you down, you have nothing left. Your whole world rises and falls on the actions of your husband. Young lady, you're not a whole person. You're just half a person. You cannot survive if you depend on someone else for your happiness. True women's liberation means finding your own happiness, in yourself, through God's power."[3]

He continued, "Marriage is not made up of two halves trying to become a whole. Rather, a marriage consists of two whole people who are bridged by the Spirit of God. Marriage never works unless each party maintains his or her own identity, settles his own values, finds his own sense of fulfillment, and discovers his own source of happiness . . . through the Lord."

Linked closely is the third fallacy of this myth. *Happiness is a result—love is a feeling.* Happiness is the result of a happening, and love is something you eagerly consume.

Both of these concepts encourage a marriage partner to be passive—to wait, to react, to see which way the ball bounces. He hopes that "something good is going to happen" to him. Many of us come to marriage shouting, "Meet my needs, love me, make me happy," and then we wait. And wait. And hope.

But the truth is that happiness is a choice. Abraham Lincoln often said, "Most people are about as happy as they choose to be." You cannot choose your feelings of happiness but you can choose the actions that will bring those feelings.

We do not do what we do because we feel the way we feel; we feel the way we feel because we do what we do. We act ourselves into a new way of feeling, not feel ourselves into a new way of acting.

We have little control over our emotions but tremendous control over our actions. That's why Erich Fromm said, "Love is not a victim of my emotions but a servant of my will." The Bible says the same, "Let us therefore practice loving."⁴ Did you ever practice anything—the piano, tennis, singing, skiing? What is practice? It is repeating the same action until you become proficient, until it becomes a part of you.

Practice has to do with actions. You can't practice feelings. Therefore, love is something you do. Eric Hoffer adds, "Love is an activity directed toward another person." Since it is action, it is a decision—a conscious act of the will, an act of faith. In the marriage ceremony a minister asks, "Will you love this person?" assuming that loving is something you can decide to do. And you answer, "Yes, I will," a promise instead of a feeling—a commitment to do instead of waiting to react. When love action is initiated toward a partner on a volitional level, the other elements of love, intellectual and emotional, will show themselves. And as John Drakeford reminds us, "Once a behavior has been established it has a momentum of its own."

So we must choose. An unhappy single will be unhappy married. An unhappy bachelor will not be changed by a wedding ring. No partner can do for me what I do not choose to desire. My happiness is my choice, not my partner's obligation.

MYTH NUMBER FOUR: "CHILDREN ARE THE GLUE"

There's a common belief that children hold a marriage together. If that were true, considering divorce statistics, they haven't succeeded too well. That would mean children of divorce are suffering for their own failures. Absurd!

A companion fable says, "Our marriage may not be too strong but the presence of children will bring a unifying focal point. If we both focus on rearing children, our own differences will go away." That's like adding a match to a powder keg and sitting on the cover.

Children don't solve marriage problems; they reveal them, aggravate them. They're very poor marriage counselors. Instead of alleviating marital strains, they magnify them. The covered fault lines will be exposed and those cute little kids will precipitate an earthquake.

Every study of marital satisfaction shows there is a decrease when children are born. By the time the third child arrives, marital satisfaction has taken a nosedive. This should not surprise us. What does a child bring to a marriage? The inescapable presence of a dependent, demanding, selfish, vulnerable creature with two ends to wipe. Certainly this is going to change the schedule, encourage frustrations, exhaust the mother, and decrease the bank balance. It will bring out the best and worst in us.

Difficulties in marriage will cause disagreement in your child-rearing approach, style, and discipline. One partner is more permissive, the other more authoritarian. One says, clamp down. The other, let go. The children caught in the middle play one parent against the other and unwittingly drive them further apart.

The primary focus must be on marriage, not on the children. We must concentrate on what we give to children, not on what they bring to us.

When Jesus said, "For this cause shall a man leave his father and mother and be joined to his wife and nothing shall separate them,"[5] he didn't say a word about children. Only marriage. Marriage is permanent, parenting temporary. We must major on the permanent, not the temporary, and bring children into a growing marriage.

Dr. Armin Grams emphasizes:

Children were never meant to be the hub of the family. Their place is on the periphery, sheltered and loved but respected as children and expected to behave that way. The center of a family is a relationship between the husband and the wife. All else revolves around that. In this way, when children leave the family, they can do so with the least disturbance of the family unit. If they are in the center of the cell, they cannot emerge without a serious rupture of the whole. Our function as parents is gradually to make ourselves unnecessary, to equip and to permit the child to orbit the family in ever-widening circles, until he establishes himself in society as a fellow adult.[6]

Even sick children can have devastating effect on a marriage. One study indicated a large percentage of divorces after a child died from a lingering illness. A mother who spends night and day nursing the child has the tendency to almost totally neglect her marriage. Soon after the funeral the decay comes to the surface and many husbands walk away. I wonder what support and care these husbands were offering during the dark days—evidently very little. Maybe they were children too.

A California study found that the marriages of a startling 80 percent of parents with children who had cancer finally broke up! Doctor Sidney Arje of the American Cancer Society concurs: "When people find themselves in this situation there are all kinds of reactions. There is a big interplay of aggressions and before you know it, many husbands and wives are chewing one another up."

"And," says Dr. M. Lois Murphey, chairman of pediatrics at a large city hospital, "if there is an emotional pathology in the family, this stirs it up. The cancer doesn't produce anything that wasn't smoldering in the first place."

So, as I have said in my book *The Marriage Affair,* a marriage begins with two people and will end the same way. It runs the cycle of parenthood and returns where it started. It starts with a couple in love, but it doesn't necessarily end that way. Often this is because of a child-centered home, and when these children are grown and gone there is no more common center of interest. These parents, in their efforts to do the best for their offspring, have actually allowed their children to come between them, to the detriment of everyone involved.[7]

These four marriage myths have one feature in common, one underlying fallacy: that you can get off the hook. That someone else—God, partner, child—is responsible for your well-being. That someone else will be the initiator.

This sets you up beautifully for an affair. If God didn't bring you the right partner, and your partner and children don't bring you happiness, why not look elsewhere? Somewhere you'll find it.

And that's a myth, too.

CHAPTER 5

Lead Me Not into Temptation

If you are thinking to yourself,
"An affair could never happen to me,"
you are in trouble.
To believe that we are immune
leaves us wide open
and unprotected.

Ellen Williams

HEN you were born you were married—married to a companion who will walk the road of life with you until the end. You will never awaken any morning or retire any night without this companion's being right at your side.

This companion will never leave you for reasons of nonsupport. You can never sue for separate maintenance. It is impossible to get a divorce. Whether you like it or not, you and this partner will be together until death do you part. Temptation—your lifelong companion.

Everyone is tempted. Temptation knows no strangers. Everyone is tempted, and always will be. No one can evade it or avoid it. It is an inescapable fact of life. If a man is alive, he is tempted. Temptation is like the dust—it falls on everyone. It is like the germs we carry with us that attack us when our resistance is down.

No isolation from people will isolate us from temptation. The priest in his secluded monastery, the hermit in his secret cave, the prisoner in his lonely cell, these all know temptation. There are no exceptions. No exemptions. Temptation is a universal, inevitable reality.

If you have a mind through which you think, you'll be tempted through that mind. If you have a body in which you live, you'll be tempted through that body. If you have a social nature by which you enjoy other people, that will be an avenue of temptation. If you are a sexual being, you'll have sexual temptations.

An author in *Psychology Today* said, "All men from the first day of their marriages onward think about the possibility of infidelity. Not that they plan to do something about it necessarily, but the possibility is a conscious thing in their minds." If the author meant that all people, men and women, face real sexual temptation, he is absolutely right. In fact, if a person thinks mistakenly that he is safe from temptation, he is already vulnerable and Satan is already greasing the skids for him.

"Never, when you have been tempted, say God sent the temptation; God cannot be tempted to do anything wrong, and He does not tempt anybody. Everyone who is tempted is attracted and seduced by his own wrong desire. Then the desire conceives and gives birth to sin, and when sin is fully grown, it too has a child, and the child is death."[1]

The Author of Temptation. During the enticement of temptation, it is easy to rationalize and make God its author. No, as James says, God does not send the temptation. To do so would be totally contrary to His nature, His objectives, and His Word.

Who tempted Adam and Even in the Garden of Eden? Who tempted Jesus for forty days in the wilderness? Satan, the devil, is called the tempter, the old serpent, and our great enemy. He prowls around like a hungry, roaring lion, looking for some victim to tear apart.[2] And he has a tremendous success pattern—having succeeded to some degree with every member of the human race.

The Nature of Temptation. Mark this well: temptation is not sin. It could never be. The Bible says, "Jesus was tempted in all points like as we are, yet without sin."[3] We used to sing the song in Sunday school many years ago: *"Yield* not to temptation, for *yielding* is sin." The temptation is not the sin.

Our reaction, our response, determines whether or not we sin. In fact, temptation all by itself is about the weakest thing in the world. All alone it is utterly powerless. To succeed, temptation always needs a partner—someone to agree with it, to dance with it, to open the door for it, to welcome it in.

You can't stop temptations from coming, but you can decide what you're going to do with each one.

You can't stop the birds from flying in the sky, but you can stop them from nesting in your hair.

You can't stop the devil from singing his bewitching songs in your ear, but you don't have to join him and sing a duet.

You can't stop the devil from displaying his wares in the shop window and urging you to buy, but you don't have to make a purchase.

You can't stop the devil from dropping his brats on your doorstep and knocking incessantly on your door. But you don't have to open the door, take them in, warm them, clothe them, and feed them.

When a girl approached me in a hotel lobby and smilingly asked, "Would you like to have a little fun tonight?" it was only a temptation. An enticement to infidelity is not sin. Our hospitality makes the difference.

Temptation Is Always to Sin . . . "and gives birth to sin," James warns. Sin is the objective of temptation. However seemingly innocent any temptation appears to be, the devil's sole purpose is to get you to sin. Not just to impede your progress a bit, to put a few hurdles in your path, but to nurse you along as a midwife and help you give birth—to sin.

The devil's objective is not to have a world full of drunkards, prostitutes, and acid heads. These are not good advertisement for him. But sin, on whatever social level, with whatever sophistication, thwarts God's wonderful plan for your life and to this sinister and destructive end, the devil is forever totally committed.

Temptation Appeals to Your Human Desires. Your God-created needs. And these are not evil. ". . . drawn away by his own desire. . . ." The appeal of temptation is always to satisfy a legitimate need in a wrong way or at a wrong time. The inner desire itself is good, to want it satisfied is fine, but how and when it is done makes the difference. The good or evil is in the way these needs are met.

Desire for friends, love, praise, success, acceptance, intimacy—these are all good. To satisfy these by dishonesty, manipulation, selfishness, and violation of God's truth leads us to sin.

Exactly so with sex. Every person is a sexual being, with sexual desires, sexual attractions, and sexual feelings. All of this is God's idea. Nothing is or ever could be wrong with sex. Because sexuality is God's gift, there can be no fault, flaw, or evil in it. But man has a history of prostituting God's gifts and using them to his selfish advantage and detriment.

Satan is sly with us. He knows that as Christians we have good taste and good motives. He does not tempt us with cheap things or brazen sin because these would not appeal to our spiritual nature. Rather, he subtly takes some very good gift of God, such as intimacy and oneness of spirit, and interjects into that gift some qualities which are not pleasing to God. He distorts our priorities and tempts us to use God's good things in the wrong place or time. Thus, sexual attraction may become a problem in a perfectly proper love relationship.[4]

Temptation Appeals to the Weakest Place in Your Life. Everyone has a special weakness. As a cunning strategist the devil marshals his strongest forces at the weakest place in the line. Our differences in temperament, personality, inherited weaknesses cause us to respond uniquely to different kinds of temptation. Peter had his special temptation, and so, certainly, did Thomas. James and John struggled with their particular weaknesses.

One person struggles every day with the temptation to steal. Another would rather die than steal. Where one person is weak, another is strong. One struggles against the temptation to lie. A girl said to me after my chapel service on the campus, "Mr. Petersen, I'm a liar. I lie all the time—always have. I've probably lied fifty times today already. I lie when I don't have to. I lie when it does me no good. But I always lied. And, by the way, I'm preparing to be a missionary." Before she becomes a missionary, she must be committed to Christ who said, "I am the truth." Someone else is strongly tempted to jealousy, swept away with envy when another succeeds or acquires position, prominence, or prestige. Another doesn't care. One person is greedy and grasping. Others have the opposite problem. They squander everything they get. Some struggle with arrogance and pride while others struggle with inferiority and pride. Sex is a bigger problem for some than others. They are more highly sexed—their emotional needs are greater. Temptation to an extramarital affair may pose a greater battle for them than for the more conservative type.

Temptation Begins in the Mind. The most important sex organ is the mind. An affair starts in the mind long before it ends up in bed. The clandestine relationship began as an innocent thought in the secret recesses of someone's mind. Thought is the source of action. The body is the servant of the mind. Thoughts determine character. Our character is cast in the mold of our concentration.

The mind is a garden that could be cultivated to produce the harvest that we desire.

The mind is a workshop where the important decisions of life and eternity are made.

The mind is an armory where we forge the weapons for our victory or our destruction.

The mind is a battlefield where all the decisive battles of life are won or lost.

The communists have learned through their brainwashing success that if they can convert and control the thoughts of people, they can reform their character and enslave them. They believe, as Emerson said, "The key to every man is his thought." Thoughts rule the world. Good thoughts never produce bad results nor evil thoughts, good results. Jesus said, "A tree is known by its fruit."

Napoleon Hill crystallized what I think is the most important and staggering concept concerning the mind. "The only thing any person has complete, unchallenged control over is his thought—his state of mind." You have no control of your circumstances or your nature; you can't control heredity or environment; you can't control your physical make-up or mental capacity, other people, friends, or enemies—the past or the future. There is only one thing you can control: you have the power to shape your thoughts and fit them to any pattern of your choice. "As a man thinketh, so is he."[5]

Thought of Evil or Evil Thought. What is the difference between them? Suppose I read a legitimate book or magazine, or watch a wholesome TV show. Something I see—an ad, a paragraph, a picture—causes a thought of evil to flash into my mind. Is that sin? No. I drive down the street and what I see on a billboard or hear on the radio causes a suggestion of evil to invade my mind. Is that sin? No. Or while I'm working on the factory assembly line, in the office lunchroom, at the club, I hear the dirty jokes, the risqué cracks, the report of sexual adventures. Is it sin for me to hear that? Of course not.

Or I meet a woman at church who is bright, charming, vibrant. Though not flirtatious, she has a radiant personality. Keeps herself in good shape, dresses well, and has an outgoing Christian kindness that makes her very attractive. A thought flits through my mind that this girl is a beauty, well endowed, and I know she is sexually attractive to any red-blooded man. Anything wrong with that? No! It is not sin to hear the hundreds of transient and tempting suggestions that knock on my mind's door every day and all life long. To the super-sensitive, the devil whispers, "There's something wrong with you. If you were a good Christian, God would be taking care of you and you wouldn't have these thoughts. It's too late; you've already sinned." You can recognize the devil's lies because they are always negative and lead to hopeless guilt and self-condemnation.

But when that passing thought of evil is welcomed, given hospitality, mulled over and over with the consent of your will, it becomes an evil thought. If I open the door, warmly invite this stranger in, give him an easy chair to relax in, and encourage additional conversation, the stranger has become my friend. This friend now helps me construct a picture—simple at first but ultimately with details and in living color—of all that this friendship can mean to me and the needs that will be met by it.

That picture is a fantasy and fantasies are a preview to the desired action. An affair is experienced many times in fantasy before the time and place of the first rendezvous is set.

Some would ask, "When Jesus taught about mental lusting or adultery, was He talking only about thoughts of evil or about evil thoughts?" Let's look carefully at his words in Matthew 5:28: "But I say to you that everyone who looks on a woman to lust for her has committed adultery with her already in his heart."

In his vibrant book *Love and Marriage,* Dr. David Hocking makes this principle beautifully clear.

First, the word "looks" is a present tense in Greek, indicating a continual habit of life. We do not believe it is saying that looking with sexual desire at a particular moment of time is wrong. God made us with sexual desire. Men enjoy looking at women and women enjoy looking at men. We believe the

*passage is condemning the practice of centering your atten-
tion on a particular person with the motive of committing
adultery with that person.*

*Secondly, the word "woman" is singular in number, not
plural. The text is not condemning the looking at women in
general, but rather the concentration on a particular woman.
A particular person begins to dominate our thinking and
desires.*

*Thirdly, the words "to lust for her" have obvious reference
to committing adultery. That is not the same as experiencing
a desire to look at a woman's physical appearance and
enjoying what you see. The problem comes when you concentrate on a particular person and mentally go to bed with her.*[6]

This is the evil thought, the fantasy, "concentrating on a
particular person and mentally planning to go to bed with
her."

At this point, the mind begins to do two things. The
subconscious part of the mind does not differentiate good
from evil and only reacts to the suggestions and pictures given
to it audibly or in the imagination. The suggestions come
from the self-talk that we all practice, often not realizing its
tremendous power and influence. Everyone engages in self-
talk all the time, unconsciously reacting to every situation,
analyzing, judging, reliving, expressing our beliefs, our fears,
our desires. Psychologist Dr. David Stoop has made a study
of self-talk and notes, "We usually speak out loud at the rate
of 150 to 200 words per minute. Some research suggests that
we talk privately to ourselves in our thoughts at the rate of
approximately 1300 words per minute. Since many of our
thoughts take the form of mental images or concepts, we can
think of something in a fleeting moment that would take us
many minutes of verbal speech to describe."[7]

As the fantasy regarding the possibility of an affair develops, our minds affirm and enhance it by what we say to ourselves and the images created. "That would be fun . . . I need that . . . life has been boring . . . she's something else . . . stolen apples are sweeter . . . I don't mean anything wrong." And so on, at 1300 words per minute. Hundreds of pictures feeding the fantasy. If we repeat any of this audibly to ourselves, that autosuggestion etches the image deeper, and our subconscious mind will work to bring it to pass.

Success motivators have long recognized the truth of this same principle. The first step to success, they say, is to decide exactly what you want to accomplish and when. Identify clearly your objective, your goal. Write this down so you can see it. Get a picture of it. Repeat the goal audibly every day, perhaps fifty times in the morning and fifty times at night. Next, make a scrapbook. Find colored pictures from magazines that relate to your goal or what you will possess once you've reached it—new house, car, smaller clothes size, vacation, etc. And as you study the pictures, engage in positive self-talk. You will create a clear, strong image in your mind; the appropriate emotions will follow, and your objective will be realized.

So our minds feed the fantasy, the fantasy creates the emotions, and the emotions scream for the actual experience. This is why when one is emotionally committed to an affair, all the truth and logic in the world don't seem to faze him. In a contest between emotion and truth, emotion usually wins.

Another thing our minds do is to deceive us. Our minds help us find what we expect to find, whether or not it is really there. We have an uncanny way of finding what we are hunting for. If we are cultivating an extramarital affair, a fantasy, our minds will come up with all kinds of ideas on *how* it can be done, *where,* and *what* the positive results will be.

Our minds also help us rationalize, that is, find good

reason to justify anything we do. We think up a nice set of reasons to justify our actions even though we may be hurting others in the process. Under the noble banner of being honest with ourselves, we deceive our partner. Our minds are not truth-finding instruments but flatter our egos and protect us from hearing things we don't want to hear. No wonder Paul talked of the need for a transformation resulting from "a renewing of our minds."[8]

When an extramarital fantasy is nurtured and has reached this point, there are several side-effects that decay the marriage further.

The Partner Becomes Passive.
It is impossible to be actively feeding a fantasy and be actively building a marriage at home at the same time. These are mutually exclusive. Attention and energy put into one are automatically taken from the other. The little things that would improve the marriage are saved for the mistress. If one initiates positive actions at home that help the relationship, he has no excuse. If the situation deteriorates further, it validates his rationalization. And certainly, there would be no serious prayer. No one is looking for God's intervention when the emotions are crying out for a warm body.

Comparison Breeds Contempt.
A partner at home in an apron is no match for one in a fantasy. Comparisons increase as the affair deepens. The spouse at home now does not communicate anymore, is not as affectionate, does not meet my needs, does not perform as well in bed, etc. In other words, she does not measure up to this dreamboat I've found. Three people are now in the bed instead of two. Sex relations, which of necessity must be perfunctory, involve only two participants but the third is in the imagination and fantasy of the cheater.

Deception Becomes the Rule.

The beginning of an affair or its continuance requires dishonesty, deceit, and duplicity. A person living a lie has no problem in telling one. In fact, the situation demands it. Lying becomes like potato chips, you can't stop with just one. Once honorable people now look their spouses straight in the eye and boldly lie about their schedules, their health, their jobs, and their expenditures. An affair cuts at the very heart of a person's integrity, and truth becomes expendable. When a person is thus involved, you believe what he does, not what he says—his actions, not his words.

A Secret Death Wish.

In order to rationalize an affair, a person's mind conjures up every conceivable subterfuge. I believe all people who have continued in extramarital liaisons have at some time wished their partners would quietly die in their sleep so they could continue their affairs without guilt. Kind of a benevolent death wish. I don't mean they want them killed—though in some cases it does involve food poisoning or a hired gun (remember David and Uriah). Nor do I mean they wouldn't honestly mourn the loss, "But if there were just some way my spouse could check out of this life legitimately and peacefully, I would be free and I wouldn't be disgraced or have to hide." The human heart, apart from the grace of God, will do whatever is necessary to twist things in accordance with its conscious or unconscious depraved desire.

WHEN TEMPTATION COMES

But it is not enough to analyze temptation—to dissect its results. How do you meet it? What do you do to pull its fangs and make it your servant?

Deflate It by Expecting It.

A great part of temptation's power is in its surprise strategy. A surprise attack is an enemy's most successful tactic. How often I've heard it from sincere Christians: "I never dreamed I'd be tempted to be unfaithful; I thought I was safe, that it couldn't happen to me." Since the Bible tells us plainly that we shall always be tempted, then why not expect it? We often play a passive, defensive game instead of an intelligent aggressive one. We express shock and surprise when temptation happens the way God said it would. The surprise would be if temptation didn't come. Why not believe Him?

A dear friend called me, and I could tell by his voice he was troubled. I didn't think much about it for I knew him to be a very strong Christian, converted from a rough life and for many years a respected leader in the church. Arriving at my office he told of a young divorcée who was destitute and how he had brought her groceries, gotten her car fixed, and tried to help her as a Christian friend. Part of her response was to become infatuated with him and invite him over for a quiet intimate evening. "I found it difficult to say no," he said. "I was surprised that there was a struggle. I guess I thought I wouldn't have those temptations anymore."

Develop a Biblical Conscience.

In a struggle with temptation we usually live our values, not our beliefs. If our conscience has been trained by the Bible and we are committed to its principles, we meet temptation with confidence instead of fear. God's warnings are the love-words of a parent telling his child not to run in the street, not to jump off the bridge, not to play with matches. They are loving protections, not arbitrary prohibitions.

Here are a few warnings that provide insight and strength—and an anchor: You will be able to resist any immoral woman

who tries to seduce you with her smooth talk, who is faithless
to her own husband and forgets her sacred vows. If you go to
her house, you are traveling the road to death. To go there is
to approach the world of death. Above all else, guard your
affections. *For they influence everything else in your life.
Spurn the careless kiss of a prostitute. Stay far from her.
Look straight ahead; don't even turn your head to look. Watch
your step. Stick to the path and be safe. Don't sidetrack; pull
back your foot from danger.*

*The lips of another man's wife may be as sweet as honey and
her kisses as smooth as olive oil, but when it is all over, she
leaves you nothing but bitterness and pain.*

*Drink from your own well, my son—be faithful and true to
your wife. Let your manhood be a blessing; rejoice in the wife
of your youth. Let her charms and tender embrace satisfy
you. Let her love alone fill you with delight.*

*Don't lust for [prostitutes'] beauty. Don't let their coyness
seduce you. For a prostitute will bring a man to poverty, and
an adulteress may cost him his very life. Can a man hold fire
against his chest and not be burned? Can he walk on hot coals
and not blister his feet? So it is with the man who commits
adultery with another's wife. He shall not go unpunished for
this sin . . . . But the man who commits adultery is an utter
fool, for he destroys his own soul.*

*"Come home with me," she urges simpletons. "Stolen melons
are the sweetest; stolen apples taste the best!" But they don't
realize that her former guests are now citizens of hell.*

*You were united to your wife by the Lord. In God's wise plan,
when you married, the two of you became one person in his
sight. And what does he want? Godly children from your
union. Therefore guard your passions! Keep faith with the
wife of your youth.*

This is why I say to run from sex sin. No other sin affects the body as this one does. When you sin this sin it is against your own body. Haven't you yet learned that your body is the home of the Holy Spirit God gave you, and that he lives within you? Your own body does not belong to you. For God has bought you with a great price. So use every part of your body to give glory back to God, because he owns it.

For God wants you to be holy and pure, and to keep clean of all sexual sins so that each of you will marry in holiness and honor. And this also is God's will: that you never cheat in this matter by taking another man's wife, because the Lord will punish you terribly for this, as we have solemnly told you before. For God has not called us to be dirty-minded and full of lust, but to be holy and clean. If anyone refuses to live by these rules he is not disobeying the rules of men but of God who gives his Holy Spirit to you.

Honor your marriage and its vows, and be pure; for God will surely punish all those who are immoral or commit adultery.[9]

Defuse It by Not Fearing It.

A fatalistic fear of temptation strengthens its power over us. Some would give anything if temptation could be eliminated and they could live without struggle. "The greatest of all temptations is the one to be without any," says Henry Drummond. Napoleon declared, "He who fears being conquered is sure of defeat."

Every temptation is an opportunity to defeat the devil. We should welcome each such opportunity. Temptation is a chance to develop virtue and mastery—a stepping-stone to building Christian character. The man who has the most temptations has the most chance of growing in grace. Limp, fragile tomato vines can be grown in the controlled atmosphere of a hothouse. But it takes winds and storms to grow oak trees. It depends on what you want to be. Every temptation drives us closer to God and gives Him a chance to confirm and demonstrate His victory over Satan.

Thank God for temptation and its beneficial effects. What the devil designs for your destruction, God uses for your development. What the devil plans for your pollution, God uses for your perfection. God uses moral struggle to bring us to maturity. God created man to have dominion, to be above circumstances, problems, temptations, not beneath them. We were made to be conquerors, not cowards—sons of God, not slaves—victors, not escapists.

Decide Irrevocably If You Want Victory.
The word "victory" implies a battle. Temptation is the battlefield. Indecision in a battle spells defeat. Your overall life purpose will determine how you meet daily temptations. If you waver here, you will vacillate when the pressure is on.

E. Stanley Jones states it graphically, "If you don't make up your mind, then your unmade mind will unmake you. Here is the place where there must be no dallying. For any dallying will be the Trojan horse that will get on the inside and open the gates to the enemy. God can do anything for the man who has made up his mind; he can do little or nothing for the double-minded."[10]

Our dear friends, broadcasters David and Karen Mains, talk about their commitment to "mental fidelity."

There are many things we do not allow ourselves to be exposed to in this wicked and foul society. Sometimes that's a conversation with someone else where we have to change the subject. Or a TV program, a magazine or newspaper that must be rejected. We can control these. People who fall sexually just don't fall automatically. They fall because they have been toying with things in their mind over a period of time. Whenever these kinds of thoughts come, we put them out of our minds. There's a tremendous force in habit, and habitually for years and years, whenever those temptations come through a magazine, billboard, or whatever, we refuse. This mental fidelity makes us unable to be violated as far as our marital relationship is concerned.

Victory doesn't just happen. It comes as a result of a total commitment to God and a planned life strategy. Nothing worthwhile is gained without a price. Surrender to God is the price you pay for freedom. Dr. Jones concludes, "A spurt of passing desire will let you down unless it gets control of your will and becomes a life desire. Vague wishing will leave you vague—and vacant. Mutually exclusive desires competing within you for the mastery will leave you cancelled out—a cipher. Make up your mind to pay the price of victory, for if you don't you'll have to make up your mind to be a house divided against itself that cannot stand." In actuality, a person doesn't step into immorality because he cannot avoid it. Rather, he does so because he inwardly cherishes a love for it. He has not made a commitment.

Determine Your Response Ahead of Time.

You cannot wait until you are nose-to-nose with temptation to decide your response. It's too late then. In the back seat of the car, at the sales convention, on the road, at the party, together in the office—these are not the places to weigh, analyze, and decide regarding an affair. There's too much emotion. The decision is made ahead of time and only confirmed at the time of temptation.

A Christian salesman friend was attending a dealers' convention in New York City. On a free evening he was waiting for a car with others to see some of the city's sights. But he got into the wrong car. These salesmen were not headed for the tourist attractions but for a famous swinging bar. Before my friend knew his mistake, they were on the way with no turning back. Upon entering the bar, each man was immediately joined by a girl who took him by the arm and led him to a table. His girl was saucy, pert, and dressed seductively. "As the evening continued, the temptation was like a steam roller," he told me later. "This girl was luscious. I had all I could do to keep from grabbing her impulsively and taking her to one of the back rooms. But the thing that held me and protected me—the only thing—was that before I had left home, I had told my wife that I was hers alone, and that regardless of any enticements, we belonged to each other and we would be praying for each other." His decision ahead of time saved him.

Discipline Your Mind with Counteraction.
Jesus told a story of a man who cleaned the evil spirits out of his house but left it clean and empty. A vacuum. Ultimately, the spirits moved back in greater force and it was worse than before. It is not enough to resist the negative—we must major on the positive. No man can long keep out evil who does not keep in good. Paul says, ". . . overcome evil with good."

Counteraction is the key. "Fix your thoughts on what is true and good and right. Think about things that are pure and lovely, and dwell on the fine, good things in others. Think about all you can praise God for and be glad about."[11] "Fix your thoughts" . . . "think" . . . "think" . . . "think." This is not shifting your mind out of gear and hoping some excellent thoughts drop in. Shift your car into neutral and it coasts downhill, out of control. Daydreaming is dangerous, one of the costliest disaster areas of life. We must deliberately, determinedly concentrate on what is pure, praiseworthy, positive, and honorable.

Our whole society discourages it. Dr. Lacy Hall conducted

a serious research project and discovered that 90 percent of the everyday input into people's lives was negative. Only 10 percent of the thoughts and concepts that came into their lives were positive. No wonder most people follow the line of least resistance and want to give up —to quit. The majority of thoughts that come into our brains and our souls are negative. This is why we must saturate our minds with the Bible and other wholesome literature. Sing songs that uplift and encourage. Find a positive Christian friend for mutual support. Thank God daily for your partner, your children, your parents, and your family.

Peter says, "Gird up the loins of your mind."[12] And Isaiah says, "Thou wilt keep him in perfect peace whose mind is stayed on thee."[13]

Discover Christ's Secret of Victory.
Our Lord was tempted in all the same ways we are, and He overcame. He met temptation as a man, using the same resources that are available to us. If He had resorted to His divine power as the Son of God, He could have worked a miracle to destroy His enemy and to provide His needs. Instead, as a human being with all the emotions, pressures, and weaknesses of man, He met the tempter at every point. For forty days in the wilderness with the wild animals He was exposed to Satan's entire arsenal of temptation. He endured forty days of severe and constant testing. For forty days and nights in the storm, the subtlety, and the persistence of temptation increased. Satan tightened the screws with every argument and enticement and was determined to make a decisive breakthrough.

The temptations came to the weakest point at the most crucial time. When Christ was famished from lack of food, the temptation was to provide bread—to satisfy the need, the hunger. When Christ was feeling forsaken, the temptation was to test God's love and see if He still cared. When Christ was overwhelmed by a sense of powerlessness, the temptation was to compromise, to gain power and dominion. At every point, Christ resisted firmly, decisively.

What was the secret of His victory? Three principles emerge:

He was obedient to His Father. Before the temptation, He had surrendered to the complete will of God. This was the underlying principle of His life—a calm, repeated choosing to obey at each advancing step. Obedience to a God-planned program for life is never easy, but it is the price of freedom and fullness.

He was filled with the Spirit. The Holy Spirit had controlled Him so the practical out-working of His commitment to God would be made possible. The power of the Holy Spirit enabled Him to face the temptation fearlessly and aggressively and come out unscathed.

He was saturated with the Scripture. To every temptation from Satan, Jesus quoted some Scripture. "It is written" was His powerful weapon in each battle. The Scripture was part of His life—memorized, studied, used.

Christ is our pattern. We gain the mastery in the same way He did, through our obedience, the Holy Spirit, and the Word of God. Our commitment and choices work in cooperation with God's power.

Two little girls were cutting through a field on the way to school. An angry bull began to chase them. One girl screamed in fright, "Let's stop here and pray that God will protect us." The other girl, a bit wiser, said, "No, we'll run and pray." Their feet and God's strength: cooperation.

Each temptation requires your responsibility and God's ability. God will not do for you what He has already equipped you to do for yourself. And no matter how hard you try, you cannot do what only He can do.

CHAPTER 6

It Happened—
Now What?

Many husbands and wives
think it is easier
to call it quits
than to repair the marriage.
When it's too late
they find they took
the easiest way out but
not the wisest.

MIDDLE-AGED MAN and his wife stood in the mud and water looking dejectedly at the ruins and rubble of their house and belongings. They were victims of a hurricane. Their lovely Texas beach home, once an enviable asset, was now a grotesque pile of stone, lumber, appliances, furniture, food, and clothing—all salt-water soaked. The storm sirens had wailed their warning, but they thought they were safe. Had they not endured other winds just as severe? And this one would be no different. The rolling waves that had been a part of their beautiful front porch view had now destroyed them.

As they gazed out at the sickening wreckage, questions they'd never asked before flooded their minds. "Do we call the Red Cross? The refuse collector? The Salvation Army? Is anything salvageable or is it worth the effort? Should we build here again; can we afford it; is it safe? Or shall we walk away from it forever?"

These are the kinds of questions that are always asked when an extramarital affair is discovered and the reality of it hits like a tidal wave. Can we build our marriage again? Do I want to? Is there anything to salvage? If so, how? Where do we begin? Can I trust again when I've been betrayed? One woman expressed her initial reaction of despair when she discovered her husband's infidelity. "Everything has come to a screeching halt. I feel like I've been stomped into the ground and I'm numb with pain. It is all so hopeless. Oh, God, help! Help me!"

Your initial and continuing reactions to your partner's affair will determine in great measure what the final results will be in pain and progress. *Infidelity may be the fact, but the feeling about that fact and your reaction to it form the crux of the problem.* Some reactions are mature but nonetheless strong. Others are totally unproductive from the start, especially from the standpoint of the marriage and family. Some reactions compound the already serious problem. Let's discuss five of the most common negative responses before we accentuate the positive. The natural human tendencies in such a stress-filled situation are to freeze, to fry, to fold, to fight, and to force.

FREEZE

This reaction makes one immobile because of refusal—a refusal to see and admit what the evidence indicates and the heart confirms. When anyone is getting involved in an affair, there are always signs, definite signs that things are not as they once were. It is not just a matter of finding a misplaced love note or lipstick on the collar. There are subtle changes in personality, attentiveness, openness, and body language.

To many, the very thought of their mate having an affair freezes them into inaction and denial. The evidence may be all around them but they will not allow themselves to accept it. If the husband came home with lipstick on his collar, they would say he probably walked under a ladder and paint dripped on him. Sally was like that. She said to me, "I kept telling myself I was making this whole thing up in my mind. It isn't happening—doesn't happen—won't happen. I'm making a big deal out of nothing." It took her more than a year to work up the courage to ask her husband one question about it.

Her unfaithful husband, meanwhile, was doing everything he could to be discovered so she would know and could help him face it. It was a cry for help. He went to the extent of saying at the breakfast table, after he'd been out all night, "I fell asleep at her house and spent the night." Still no questions, no confrontation. Sally was burying her head in a pillow of fantasy, feeling somehow that thinking about the problem would encourage it—that the thing she feared might come upon her.

One mistress wondered aloud if this kind of wife could be the innocent party. "I asked my lover if his wife is aware of our relationship. Does she know?"

"She doesn't want to know," he said. "She never asks. If she did, I would tell her."

The woman went on, "In affairs like this, there are no innocent parties. Only human ones who don't ask questions because they don't want to know the answers."

Linda Wolfe, who has written much on marital infidelity, says it clearly. "Denial is a psychological device that permits a woman to pretend to herself that her husband is perfectly faithful, even when he goes out of his way to give her evidence of his infidelity. In a typical case, a deny-er manages to hold onto her marriage even when the marriage is nothing but a farce."[1]

Denial is an escape mechanism based on fear, false hope, and a lack of trust in God. There is a fear of inadequacy for this crisis, a sense of having no resources, not knowing where to turn in this confusion. So feelings of helplessness, loneliness, and despair sweep over you and you cannot face the demands of the difficulty. "I cannot allow myself to believe this for I wouldn't know what to do if it were really true." Thoughts of suicide are often common at this point. Sally, whom I mentioned earlier, told me how, during her denial, she worked harder, drove herself literally day and night— some nights having only three hours sleep—to get this out of her mind. On the verge of a breakdown, she overdosed on sleeping tablets so she wouldn't have to cope, thinking, "The only solution is not to feel at all."

Sally's case may seem extreme, but any kind of denial only encourages and aggravates the problem. Denial produces several disastrous courses of action:

You begin unconsciously to cover for your partner, make excuses for his actions, take the blame yourself for his behavior. You become part of the problem, not the solution. When your children or your parents comment or question, you're quick to pretend, to alibi, to rationalize it away. "He's been working too hard . . . hasn't gotten enough sleep lately, etc., etc."

You unwittingly encourage the affair. Time in this case does not heal, it only rewards the deceptor with greater opportunity. Passive denial gives the affair opportunity to deepen until recovery may be impossible and the marriage is doomed.

You prolong the punishment and keep God from actively bringing solutions. Even God Himself is limited if no one admits the truth. God doesn't work in some strange, ethereal way in the atmosphere around the problem. He works in and through people—through someone who initiates, confronts, forgives, heals.

You refuse to love. Being frozen in a position of inaction also says to a straying partner that you don't care, that your love is thin, based on your convenience. Tough love says, "I cannot let you go on hurting yourself and others and missing God's dream for you."

In a true story about an anonymous couple, Ellen Williams graphically describes a woman's struggle with her minister husband. "Twice in the months that followed, I asked him. Lying beside him in our bed—tight, stiff, trembling, working up the courage. 'Is there someone else?'

"'No!' he said with anger in his voice, giving me the only answer I wanted to hear. I curled myself around his back, this man I knew so well, this man I had married twenty-seven years ago, and we went to sleep, knowing he had lied to me. I heard it in his voice, felt it in his body. I did the only thing I knew to do when something is too scary to face. I turned my back on it. If I didn't look, maybe it would go away."[2]

FRY

Many betrayed partners burn inside; they fry with self-pity and self-righteousness. There is hostility and humiliation also, but it expresses itself in a "look what he did to me" attitude. In discovering her husband's affair, Lorna explained in shocked disbelief, "After all I've done for him and this is his thanks! I've given him the best years of my life. I've had his children. Kept the house clean for him. Cooked his meals. Had a clean shirt for him every morning. I've stood by him in the tough times, and now I'm not good enough for him. That's gratitude for you." And she could have probably ticked off dozens of other good things she had done for him. She had a no-nonsense personality and a tendency to take the reins and direct family activities and chores with a kind of top-sergeant crispness. She often barked out orders instead of asking for help. Her idea of a good time was "doing something constructive," like digging a large garden plot or making six pairs of curtains in an evening.

Lorna was a good woman, but her sense of worth was wrapped up in her accomplishments. She assumed that these would also build their marriage relationship, and when they didn't, she was offended and depressed, and she lashed out against the unappreciative spouse.

My friend Bob was not only succeeding in his auto sales business but had the image to go with it. He liked fine clothes, good cars, a swimming pool, and all the extras. The inside of his home was immaculate, manicured, and always appeared as if no one lived there. I had visited there many times. When he discovered his wife's affair, he was amazed. He exclaimed in disbelief, "I gave her everything she wanted—clothes, car, money—I redecorated the house, bought new furniture. Now she's ruined my reputation, taken advantage of me. I guess it's true that you can never understand or please a woman."

Self-esteem

Wounded pride is closely related to a person's self-esteem and self-image. The fact that a partner has found someone more attractive shatters that self-esteem. A feeling of worthlessness, even self-hate, sets in. One wife exclaimed, "I began to feel ugly, horribly so, and I stood in front of the mirror examining myself to see what was wrong that made me so undesirable." Evelyn Miller Berger tells of another wife who knew that her negligence in putting on extra weight encouraged her husand's affair, and the self-loathing that followed almost destroyed her. "My husband complained about my being overweight. He asked me how I could expect him to be sexually excited when my body felt like an overstuffed pillow. I tried to reduce but the criticisms made me want to eat more—a sort of solace. But I think, too, I was angry then for his blaming me and I thought, 'Well, if you don't like it, I'll just show you I can eat to get as fat as I please!' Then I knew I *was* downright ugly—fat—and I loathed myself."[3]

One betrayed wife felt her reputation was devastated. "I felt I could not leave the house again. What will my neighbors, my friends, the people at church think now? This says to everyone that I cannot hold my husband. It isn't fair," she wailed. "How can he expect me to look glamorous when I have children and a house to look after?"

Perfectionism

A pride-martyr response is usually the uppermost reaction from a perfectionist when the partner is unfaithful. The perfectionist is a frightened, competitive individual who always wants to win, to dominate and control those around him. He is often a chronic fault-finder and nothing is ever good enough. As a Christian, he is legalistic. He likes the rules, rituals, and standards, and cannot live spontaneously. Fearful of intimacy, he makes his marriage more of a business contract than a freeing love-affair. Sex becomes a perfunctory obligation. There is little fun and laughter.

When the husband was playful and flirtatious, one such wife remonstrated, "George, stop that. We're not kids anymore." He ultimately found someone who did enjoy his winks and caresses. And his wife was horrified. In counseling her my wife asked, "How often did you have sex with your husband?" She was a bit embarrassed but answered pensively, "I think the last time was on his birthday... yes... I gave him sex on his birthday." An annual present. When my wife told me, I said it was a good thing he wasn't born on February 29 in leap year.

She played the martyr's role well, and enjoyed it. In addition, she thought she was a well-taught, advanced Christian and had serious doubts that her husband was one at all. Thus, his affair and subsequent divorce were part of her being "persecuted for righteousness sake." Of course, that had nothing to do with it, but to elicit sympathy, that's what she broadcast. She still believes her loneliness is the price she pays for being righteous, and this only increases her isolation.

FOLD

The mate who folds falls in a pile and takes all the blame, waiting for the inevitable. To fold, Webster defines, is to "close for lack of funds—to weaken or collapse from exertion." In other words, to declare bankruptcy, to admit that your resources are totally depleted, to throw in the towel, to relinquish control, to become a victim. How descriptive these phrases are of reactions to the discovery of adultery.

The Leaner

Some, especially women, fall in a pile because of being leaners. The wife's prop is taken away and she falls. The one person she has been totally dependent upon, her crutch, has been removed and she cannot stand. Suddenly she is aware she feels deprived, weak, defenseless, inadequate, and frightened, as if she'd suddenly lost her power to meet life. The future seems dangerous, foreboding. The unresolved habit of leaning has left her unable to support herself, physically and emotionally.

Mary, a very religious type, came to me for counsel. She was a frightened little girl, although she had been married sixteen years. Her husband, Bill, had asked for a divorce so he could continue his affair with Dottie. Mary was visibly shaken—devastated. Dottie was a young thing in his office, plagued by home problems with her husband, and Bill had become her "comforter." The whole thing came as a blockbuster even though Mary told me she'd been hearing of Dottie and her problems with her "dog" of a husband every day. "I had Dottie for breakfast, for lunch, and dinner and though I was sick and tired of hearing of her, I didn't expect any infidelity."

Bill's demand for a divorce knocked out all her supports and she caved in. Of course, he played her like a violin. He threatened to leave—even packed his clothes—and she begged him back. He threatened to sell the house from under her and, as he expected, she folded, tearfully pleading for mercy. Just like a slave. Her dependency degraded her and he actually hated her for it. "I hate myself," she said, "for being so immature that I had to lean on anybody so much I'd be completely lost when left on my own." The situation changed dramatically when she experienced a conversion to Christ and through His strengthening power began initiating positive action.

The Abused
Some are rendered hopeless by sheer violence and abuse. A petite, well-educated, and gifted church friend, Naomi, was paralyzed by fear of bodily harm. "If I faced my husband with his deception and unfaithfulness," she told me, "I am sure he would stop at nothing to make me and the children pay dearly." I met him. He was a big and angry man—a bully. In spite of all my urgings to help her develop a strategy of action, she couldn't. He had her petrified.

The Guilty
Guilt also paralyzes, probably more than any other one reaction. Often the rejected partner looks inward and takes all the blame for the whole sordid mess. This introspection is not the healthy questioning which asks if one has contributed in any way to the situation and acknowledges and learns from any failure. Rather it is looking for a scapegoat, someone on whom to place all the blame. And because of his own insecurities, he assumes total responsibility. As the TV commercial used to say, "I ate the whole thing." This is neither true nor helpful.

The rejected wife often reviews all the things she should have done differently and dwells on her past mistakes—some real and some imaginary. The more she analyzes her past, the more reason she finds for her predicament. Her sense of self-worth takes a nose dive; her guilt multiplies—false guilt, much of it. The devil will keep some people from ever taking an honest inventory; others he pushes overboard and drowns them in false self-condemnation.

One wife wrote to a counselor in a Christian magazine,

"My husband told me he loved another woman. At first I was angry but now I feel like it was all my fault. I feel that as a Christian I should have done more to save my marriage. I didn't give enough. I didn't love enough. I feel like a failure as a wife and as a woman. Some mornings I can barely drag myself out of bed. I'd rather sleep and forget. Is there hope?"

Another said, "I can't stop dwelling on my mistakes. I feel like the black sheep, for our family's never had affairs before."

As if every aspect of the marriage depended on her, another broken spouse confessed, "I failed as a mother as well as a wife because I didn't train our children so my husband would want to spend his time with them in our home." Since this woman evidently believed that her husband had no responsibility for the training of the children or the atmosphere of the home, she would surely not be able to allow him to take any responsibility for his adulterous affairs. In this way, she encouraged them.

The Escapist

Another word that would be synonymous with "fold" in this setting would be "flee." The natural tendency is to run when you're frightened and not sure where you are or what to do. Giving in or giving up is a way of fleeing, of running away. The escapism may prompt a refusal to consider forgiveness, an explosive retaliation, or a quick divorce. But whatever renders one immobile or unable to act is unhealthy and nonproductive.

Some Christians fold in the face of an affair because of their own distorted and anemic Christian faith. Their brand of Christianity makes them doormats to be trampled and walked over. They have no right to ask questions regarding evil, but must endure it passively and suffer silently. They do not allow themselves to deal with the infidelity, but just go along with it and, if need be, accept a life of extreme humiliation.

The problem with all this inaction is that it rewards the unfaithfulness and prolongs its resolution. Extramarital affairs are resolved with some kind of action strategy and you can't initiate action from the bottom of the pile.

FIGHT

I'm sure that there has never been an extramarital affair where anger was not evident—anger from the one who is unfaithful, for the real or supposed negligence that prompted his infidelity, and anger, certainly, from the one who feels betrayed. No matter how calm or understanding one seems on the surface, there is some outrage smoldering within or preparing to blow everything sky-high. There is anger over the embarrassment, the humiliation, the disillusionment, the deception.

One woman I read of flared when she discovered her husband's affair. "I threw a plate at him. I told him he could just walk straight out the door, that I didn't want any man who didn't want me. 'I don't want to walk out,' he said. 'I love you; I love the kids.' That made me even madder; in fact, I threw a glass at him." That gave her a little relief but it certainly didn't resolve anything. And dishes are expensive.

It would be unhealthy if there were no anger against the "terrible psychological violence of adultery." Linda Wolfe says, "Psychoanalysts call adultery a 'psychic injury' and indeed there does seem to be something almost viscerally-piercing about it. It is not only a sharp wound to the ego but also to the trust between lovers—a wound that can and often does end by bleeding a marriage to death."[4]

But why this anger is expressed, and in what form, determines whether or not it is destructive. Are we fighting for the marriage, against the evil, against the partner, or for the purely selfish reasons of our hurt feelings? The fight may take several forms:

Retaliation is as common as it is self-defeating and useless. Though the New Testament writers mention several times, "Not repaying evil for evil," yet this is a very human tendency. "If he can do it, I can too." Many wives yield to the desire to get even, to give him a taste of his own medicine, to prove they're still desirable and can get a man—out of spite.

Evelyn Miller Berger tells of one woman she counseled. "I felt justified in doing some playing around," the client said with open hostility. "I wanted some attention too. But when the affair was over, I suddenly woke up to the fact that I'm that despicable character, the Other Woman, me! Imagine that! Good, steady, old daughter of a professor, always such a good little girl on the straight and narrow path of virtue."[5] Even though there is an undeniable selfish pleasure in getting even, yet it only compounds the problem—doubles it. Now there are two who have gone astray and need forgiveness.

The most important insight is, who is in control? If you return evil for evil—your *reaction* determined by your partner's *action*—your partner controls you. To respond in kind is to be controlled by the person initiating the action. You are controlled by the person whose actions you copy. You cease to be an initiator and become only a reactor, and the whole thing backfires. You are no more innocent in the whole affair than your husband or the Other Woman.

Revenge is more than retaliation. It is committed to finding a way to punish in return for the injury inflicted. A straying husband may not be hurt at all when his wife has her "fling" in retaliation for his. He may be glad. He now has a good reason for walking out. But if she wants to avenge herself for her suffering, she will make sure he suffers too.

One divorcée wrote to "Dear Abby" after her husband's affair. "I behaved like a maniac. I screamed and carried on. I packed his clothes and ordered him out of the house. Then I made a fatal mistake. I told our relatives and friends and went immediately to a lawyer and filed for divorce. I created such a public scandal that my husband could no longer stay in town." She evened the score and got revenge. But did it work? "I realize now that I was thinking only of myself. My children paid the price for my pride. They were three boys, all under ten years of age." She continues, "The years have gone by. My sons are married now and gone, but I am lonely and miserable and my bitterness shows."[6]

Blame. Anger takes another form: blame. The opposite of the one who accepts all the blame, whom I mentioned earlier, is the one who *assigns* all the blame. She explodes in self-righteous wrath and waits for her husband's confession and return. One woman boiled over to me, "It's his problem, not mine. I get tired of these questions . . . 'Where did *I* fail? Where did *I* go wrong? How did *I* neglect him? etc., etc.' He had the affair; I didn't. And for the record, let me say, I didn't push him into her bed. He climbed in on his own."

There's also the desire to fight the "third party." "That hussy stole my husband and she's going to pay for it." If the other woman is a stranger, you may have an overwhelming desire to confront her and kill her with your words. Doris was such a woman. She demanded that her husband reveal who this "worm" was. Upon his refusal she had him followed. Later, when she drove to the house to "see who her competition was," she was unbelieving. The house was simple, small, in a very ordinary neighborhood—in stark contrast to the large home and the beautiful well-treed subdivision their success had brought them. She rang the doorbell and waited nervously. When the door opened, there was no voluptuous raving beauty framed in the doorway. Only an unkempt, frumpy young housewife!

After Doris had verbally abused and consigned this woman to perdition, she demanded that her husband not be allowed to visit her again. The reply she got brought her little comfort. "If your husband comes back or stays away, that is his decision. I cannot control that. Perhaps he's finding something here he's not getting at home."

If the "other woman" is a neighbor, friend, or social acquaintance, you fight in a different way: with slander—at the beauty shop, the neighborhood coffee klatch, the church, the Bible class. She is methodically destroyed by that "little member," the untamed tongue, which James says is full of deadly poison.

FORCE

Forcing means to charge, to push impetuously for a solution, to manipulate the people involved and the situation for a quick fix. It is natural that we want to get rid of an ugly problem as soon as possible. No emotionally healthy person wants to prolong the pain one minute longer than he has to. If you have a tendency to be a "take-charge" person, it is almost impossible for you to sit back and wait for solutions to emerge and ripen. It is almost as if you believe that any action is better than no action.

The uncovering of an affair triggers so many conflicting emotions—the surprise of it, the deception, the disappointment, the betrayal. Something must be done. Like a drowning man, you thrash the water wildly, hoping to lay hold of something that will be your rescue. The miracle.

These desperate actions may be totally unrelated, even

contradicting each other. Or they may range from conniving and manipulating circumstances to quoting Scripture.

A fine Christian friend of ours, Judy, was devastated by her husband's chronic affairs and their subsequent divorce. I asked her what reaction she had that turned out to be negative, unproductive. "I did everything spiritual I could think of to force the situation to a head. I said to my husband, 'Let's pray about it,' and expected a miracle. I quoted Scripture to him—verses that he knew as well as I did since we both had a Christian background. I repeated all the Christian clichés and pat formulas.

"Then after all my preaching didn't work, I sent a Christian worker to talk to him, to use his spiritual 'magic' on him. When all of these spiritual formulas only compound the problem, you begin secretly to lose your faith in God, too."

"What other things, of a nonspiritual nature, were you tempted to do?" I inquired.

"Well, there is the tendency to let your partner know you'd be destroyed without him, so his guilt is increased. Also, you want to spy on him, manipulate him in an attempt to keep them apart, or try to intervene in a dramatic rescue. I learned the hard way," Judy declared with great conviction, "that these kinds of efforts not only failed but actually worsened the situation."

These five reactions—freeze, fry, fold, fight, force—lead to a dead end. Negative reactions always do. They have one thing in common—they provide the partner a transient bit of self-satisfaction, but they do not contribute to resolving the dilemma. They only aggravate an already sensitive and volatile matter.

A little boy was asked by his father to say grace at the table. While the rest of the family watched, the little guy eyed every dish of food his mother had prepared. After the examination he bowed his head and honestly prayed, "Lord, I don't like the looks of it, but I thank you for it and I'll eat it anyway. Amen." The right response in a tough situation.

That is the next important chapter.

CHAPTER 7

Untangling the Triangle

*I have yet to know
of a marriage threatened
with the intrusion
of a third party
where each partner had not
contributed to the triangle.*

Dr. Evelyn Miller Berger

HE SUSPICION and the discovery of an extramarital affair can be a wrenching emotional experience. Emotions of surprise, shock, anger, fear, hate, and blame come cascading over you like a Niagara. You become confused, and instead of your reactions being planned and positive they are unpredictable and explosive. Sociologist Lewis Yablonsky notes that when an affair is discovered, men are likely to be self-righteous and angry, less likely to see the affair as an act against them, and tend to take action. Women are likely to be hurt; they absorb the news and wonder what's wrong with them, they reexamine the relationship, and tend finally to let the infidelity pass.

It certainly is difficult to think logically and sensibly when your marriage, like the *Titanic,* has hit an iceberg and you feel as if everything you've lived for is sinking out of sight. No wonder our reactions are often frantic and implusive. It is impossible to sit quietly on the tilting deck and map out a strategy for rescue.

However, there is a difference between the *Titanic* quickly sinking to the bottom of the ocean and a marriage gashed by an affair. Marriage is a relationship, not an object. Relationships are neither developed nor destroyed in a moment as a result of one experience, good or bad. They grow or deteriorate from many experiences and our reaction to those experiences. Therefore, a panic effort is unnecessary as well as unproductive.

"So your partner has strayed?" asks counselor Evelyn Miller Berger. "That does not mean that your life is ruined, that your purpose for living is gone; there is something you can do about it. It may call on your greatest inner resources but even if you fail to save your marriage there yet can be deep meaning to life, and with wisdom and patience you may even save your marriage."[1] An affair is really quite a complex thing and doesn't yield to simple one-shot solutions. It did not begin overnight; it will not be solved overnight. We can and must develop an effective coping strategy because both the injured and the guilty parties are swamped with uncertainties about how to behave.

I have isolated ten practical principles that will provide us a better understanding of ourselves, the problem, and the solutions. These will help where the affair has just been discovered or where it has been going on for a long time. Even for those not personally affected in any way by an affair at the present time, these principles will be part of an affair-prevention strategy. These are not listed in any order of importance or sequence, but the first four will, I hope, come before the last six.

TAKE TIME BEFORE YOU TAKE ACTION

This may be the toughest and most difficult thing to do, but it will certainly be the wisest. To protect yourself from snap judgments and snapping emotions you must back off from the situation instead of rushing into it. "The most important thing to do immediately is nothing," says Dr. Rita R. Rogers, professor of psychiatry at UCLA. "Don't flee into action, but rather retreat into reflection. Evaluate what it all really means to your partner as well as to you."[2] The tendency upon discovering infidelity is to accuse, blame, threaten, panic. There is no way this kind of approach can be constructive, because you are acting out of your emotions and these can fluctuate wildly when you are suffering the unbearable pain of a breaking heart. Wounded pride, jealousy, and righteous wrath will urge you to some explosive action. Resist that.

Don't immediately go out and do something drastic, such as hurrying to the lawyer, filing for divorce or threatening separation, or issuing some on-the-spot ultimatum that forces your partner to take hasty action that will make it impossible to repair the marriage.

If you take impulsive and immediate action, you will never be able to understand what really happened and why. Wait until you know what is going on with your partner before you take any rash or ill-conceived measures. Instead, you must give yourself time to let your emotions settle. This may take days; if so, take the time. But resist every temptation to do something quickly or to have a showdown. Don't talk to anyone yet for advice or sympathy. One day the tears scald your face and you feel like you could cry forever, and the next day you will feel totally destroyed—aching all over or numb with pain.

Another suggestion: Don't hurry away on a separate vacation because you "need time to think it through." This only invites more involvement with the "other woman." Maintain your regular routine; keep active physically, keep the house clean, care for the children. Don't give up your responsibilities at home, at church, or in the community, except perhaps for a brief period of rest and relaxation. If you work outside the home, stay on your job. This is important to your healing and self-esteem.

This is the time to talk to God. Pour out your heart to Him and tell Him exactly how you feel. He knows your humanness. Do not tailor your words to fit your notion of Him. He will not be shocked or upset. Spread the whole thing out before God and ask for His wisdom. He is a very present help in trouble. One rejected woman wrote a counselor, "I prayed for the patience not to lose my temper and weep or criticize, the way I felt like doing. I prayed for help to go on loving instead of hating my husband as I was beginning to do. I had a hard time forgiving him for what he had done, so I prayed about that, too."

Another anonymous woman told of the important insight she received as she prayed. "My first help on that shocking day was prayer. Just communicating with God lifted some of my anxiety, but it did more than that. In prayer I came to realize on an emotional level the truth that I had formerly known only academically. Faced with the possibility of a fractured family and divorce, I learned forcefully that Christian marriage is more than a legal contract between a man and woman or an agreement that can be brought to an end whenever the wife or husband finds it convenient."

She continued, "I reasoned that God was present when we married; He must be present now when we are facing trouble. This gave me comfort. Then I carried my reasoning further. My husband and I both had a stake in our marriage; God also had a stake in our marriage. 'That's two against one,' I thought wryly, putting God—very self-righteously, I realize now—on my side. Then mentally, I carried my logic a step further. God, myself, three children, and something I called home and family—all these were balanced against one man and one woman in a state of romantic love. Who could logically compare the tragedy of a broken romance to that of a broken marriage?"

Taking time for reflection and prayer in the early stages of affair-discovery is the most important action you can take. Believe that somehow God will give you wisdom and bring good out of a negative situation.

SEPARATE THE FACTS FROM YOUR OPINIONS

When an affair is discovered, the mind of the betrayed goes into high gear. Not only is every kind of emotion experienced, but these emotions are fleshed out in your thoughts day and night. You unconsciously mix the actual facts with your negative opinion of those facts, and create a false picture of yourself and of the difficulty. Not only do you rehearse the facts themselves over and over in your mind but you interpret those facts and come to conclusions. When your interpretations and conclusions are added to the bare facts, you come up with a totally distorted and inaccurate picture.

Now, certainly it is not easy to think logically and accurately when you are under this kind of stress and upheaval. But it is absolutely essential to force yourself to think clearly or your emotions will run wild and spawn every kind of untruth. I am not saying your emotions are right or wrong, but they cannot be in the driver's seat. You must constantly differentiate between what are the real facts and what are negative opinions you have unconsciously mixed with the actual facts. For example: The fact is, "My partner is unfaithful," but you may add a false and negative conclusion: ". . . therefore he doesn't care for me and the children anymore."

"My husband loves another woman."	—therefore, "I have lost my beauty and am now ugly."
"My partner deceived me."	—"I can never trust him again."
"I've been betrayed."	—"Our love can never be rekindled. It will always be cold and barren."
"I've been hurt so deeply."	—"I can never forgive and be healed."
"This is the first affair in our family."	—"Our reputation is ruined."

"Our marriage has failed."	—"I'm a failure as a wife and mother."
"This is the first affair in our church."	—"Christian people will not accept us now."
"Our family is fractured."	—"Our children will be marked for life."
"I have committed adultery."	—"God will not forgive. I will be a second-class Christian now. God cannot use me anymore; I'm finished."

None of these deductions is valid. The facts are true—the conclusions are false. And because such conclusions are always negative, they destroy your self-esteem and plunge you into hopeless despair. Failure of the marriage becomes your failure and renders you immobile and guilt-ridden. It also says you believe failure is fatal and final; therefore, there is no reason to believe and aggressively work toward a solution.

DON'T LET THE PRESENT DESTROY THE PAST

The disappointment and deception of an affair significantly change the present but in the process they may also discolor the past, or steal it away from you altogether. The distress you are suffering now causes you to wonder if all the marriage and family joys of the past were phony and your partner a hypocrite. There is a tendency to think, "He has always deceived me; he never did love me, didn't mean the things he said." So we lose perspective on the good experiences of the past. The disagreements and difficulties of the past are magnified, exaggerated, and nothing looks good anymore.

Ellen Williams quotes an unnamed wife who wrote after her husband's affair:

We recognized our marriage had been good. This was easier for my husband to affirm than for me. I had a tendency to discount the entire fabric of our years together because of one spot, as though something that had occurred in the present could negate the goodness of the past. We began to recall those years both in the heat of our arguments and in our more quiet times. Our life together had a rich history of shared experiences, three children, and a little grandchild. All of this was put on one side of the scale. It far outweighed the unhappiness of the past year.[3]

So, treasure the good times you had—the enjoyment of each other, the laughter, the comfort, the intimacy. Of course, there will be stabs of pain when you think of these things in the light of the present betrayal. But let the positive experiences of the past encourage you to work for a present solution. Don't sacrifice the pleasure of the past to the failure of the present. Don't cancel the past. Cherish it. Build on it.

COMMIT YOURSELF TO LEARN—NOT TO LEAVE

Discovery of an extramarital affair immediately brings a painful reassessment process. The dynamics between you and your partner will undoubtedly and irrevocably be changed. The relationship will never be the same again. And two questions are always asked, either deliberately or unconsciously, by both the innocent and guilty partner. "Should I leave? Should my partner leave?" And dozens of other questions are wrapped up in those two: "What should I do?" "What will be the outcome?" "Can I trust again?" "Whose fault is it?" etc., etc.

You are ill-prepared to answer those questions in your dazed condition. But you can decide whether for you this tragedy will be the end of a marriage or the beginning of a learning process. After Adam and Eve had disobeyed God and were found out, they immediately blamed God, the devil, each other, and the situation. They chose to blame—not to listen; to lash out—not to learn; to hide—to protect themselves from the disapproval of God and those they loved. All men ever since have had the same basic struggle. Dr. Ruth Neubauer, New York marriage and family therapist, says, "Reconstruction of a marriage depends in large measure on how quickly a couple can move beyond the stages of simply assigning blame. Partners who never move beyond the blaming stage may stay married, but the problems that led to the affair in the first place go unexamined and may result in a cycle of repeated infidelities."[4]

No friend of God or of marriage says an affair is a desirable thing. But an affair is a crisis that pinpoints a need, an indication a change is necessary—a change-point. Counselor Marcia Lasswell confirms, "The person involved in an affair has made an undeniably dramatic statement that cannot be ignored, and has opened up the possibility for the couple to do constructive work on the relationship."[5]

Psychologist Dr. Ruth K. Westheimer concurs. "I would never recommend an affair ... because the other consequences are too painful. Nevertheless, it is a fact that some spouses are jolted out of their complacency by a partner's affair."[6] One jolted, betrayed wife confessed, "Every time I think of those terrible days, I resolve again to treat my marriage and my husband with more care."

Infidelity is more often a symptom than a cause of marital fracture. Just like the oil light in your car, the flashing light reveals a problem that must be taken care of immediately—a symptom of a major difficulty. The red light does not indicate the car has never been any good, a lemon from the factory. Nor does it indicate the car is ruined and you should call the wrecker. It is a signal, a warning that some important action is necessary. Many years ago my wife was driving along contentedly and the red light on the dash began flashing. Not knowing for sure what it indicated, but thinking it might signal some minor adjustment, she kept on driving, even faster, to find a garage. By the time she got to the garage, miles away, the whole engine was shot. Had she interpreted the signal correctly, the results would have been positive.

The affair is an indicator—an alarm, a catalyst for positive change. Determine you are going to learn from it and not use it as a pretext to cop out, give out, or walk out. Even if your efforts are not successful and divorce ensues, you can still learn much that you would not learn any other way. God uses all things—all that we let Him—to teach and to temper us, even the disaster of a fractured marriage.

DETERMINE THE FACTS
BEFORE DECIDING THE FATE

Affairs come in all sizes and shapes and for various reasons. The setting and causes are different in each case, as different as the people involved in them. There is no one "typical" affair. Says Dr. Westheimer, "There are many kinds of affairs begun for different reasons with varying degrees of seriousness."[7]

Though adultery is involved in both a one-night stand and a long-term affair, the dynamics and results vary and each must be handled in a different way. The Bible college dean I counseled who determinedly seduced every girl he could on campus is one thing. A close friend of mine, who, rebounding from a marriage problem, yielded to one experience one night and then confessed it to God and to his wife is another thing.

The Bible makes a difference between one who is overtaken in a fault—who falls because of unwatchfulness or the violence of temptation and then gets up—and the one who continues on a planned program of sinning, only regretting that he was caught. This is not to say that the one is less a sinner than the other, nor is it meant to minimize the sin, but it means only that the counseling and counter-action are different. I might add here, the chronic adulterer—whose infidelity is a way of life—is generally a man whose behavior had little to do with his wife or the quality of his marriage. Apart from a miracle of God he is not likely to change.

In his enlightening book *Affair Prevention,* Episcopal minister Peter Kreitler lists eight common types of extramarital affairs: The Friendship Affair, the Be a Good Neighbor Affair, the Cup of Coffee Affair, the Seize the Moment Affair, the Old Acquaintance Never-to-be-forgotten Affair, the People Helper Affair, the Western Affair, and the Office Affair. The names he's given to these tell how or where they begin and are quite self-explanatory, except perhaps the Western Affair. This involves the promiscuous man whose many affairs are like notches on his masculinity belt—as a cowboy might cut notches in his gun stock for every bad guy killed.[8]

You cannot treat a sickness unless you know what kind it is. One study showed that 31 percent of the women involved voluntarily told their husbands about their affairs, compared with only 17 percent of the men. Therefore, there must come a time for open discussion and fact-finding. This direct discussion is to determine the basic facts of the case—the kind of affair, who is involved, the duration, the level of commitment your spouse has to his or her love. Also, it is important to know your partner's feeling about the affair and the future of your marriage. No accusations, hysteria, threatening, blaming, or probing for details. This initial confrontation may well indicate whether there is any possibility that the marriage can survive.

Before the actual discovery of the affair you probably saw some of the signs, so you already have some information. There were changes in his habits or in your established marriage patterns—or an uncharacteristic interest in his personal appearance or a disinterest in sex, even impotency. Or a revived interest in sexual experimentation, or frequent unexplained changes in his work schedule or leisure time. Or a drift into silences.

Dr. Richard Fisch, professor of psychiatry at Stanford University Medical School, suggests this:

If you want to repair your marriage instead of dumping your husband, don't try to get him to confess the adultery through questioning, innuendo, or other forms of entrapment. Tell him straight out that you know . . . and how you know. Also, wait until the first emotional shock is over before you try to talk about it at all. When at last you do broach the subject, don't use threats, such as divorce or separation, don't keep reminding him that you feel betrayed, that he has forever lost your trust. And don't insist that he goes for professional help.[9]

During this first discussion, was he relieved that the problem was out in the open? Did he want to talk? Did he express regret that you were hurt or indicate a desire to make the marriage work? These are all good signs and should be encouraged. It provides a golden opportunity to use your best wisdom, and the chances are reasonably good that you will be able to save your marriage.

But perhaps he was secretive, denying, excusing, blaming, defiant. This makes the challenge greater but not necessarily impossible. Your sensitive and carefully considerate responses to this initial confrontation will be most significant.

Your only purpose here is to get the facts, not to jump to conclusions or to initiate action.

ASK FOR REASONS, NOT FOR DETAILS

Once you get the honest facts you must explore the reasons for the infidelity—reasons that will help you understand the causes and how you are involved. Why has your husband turned to another woman? What are his struggles? In almost every instance of marital infidelity, the "other woman" is providing something the wife is not giving. Your motive must be to learn and comprehend, not to defend yourself or assign blame—to confront with care, not with criticism—to listen without malice or anger. This may be the toughest assignment of all—to listen, to put yourself in your partner's shoes, to try to understand his feelings and why he believes the affair took place. Some of the things you hear will be hard to take. They may reflect upon you. You may be hurt, even wrongly accused. One woman told me her husband said, "I can't talk to you and I just needed someone to talk to." You may feel unjustly criticized. But bite your lip, wipe away the tears, and listen—*listen!* No belittling, no moralizing, no sermons, no Bible verses.

I'm not suggesting a practical impossibility, that an offended partner sit passively expressing no feelings, repressing all pain. This may be the time when you tell how deeply you have been hurt and begin to establish guidelines for rebuilding trust between you. But if you yourself are bitter and see nothing but fault and belittle an already guilt-ridden partner, it can be disastrous. Dr. John F. O'Connor of Columbia Psychoanalytic Center for Training and Research adds this suggestion: "When telling, use the 'I' rule. Say, 'I was hurt,' rather than 'You hurt me.' In other words, never start a sentence in a conversation by putting the partner on the defensive. Both of you should try to think, 'This is a dumb thing to do to our marriage,' and try to think of being in the situation together."[10]

A family therapist at Northside Hospital in Atlanta, Georgia, Dr. Alfred A. Messer, comments, "Every wife confronting adultery should insist that her husband sever all connections with the other person and concentrate on enhancing their own marriage satisfaction. Discovery diminishes the power of an affair. It loses its clandestine attraction and becomes less appealing and less meaningful."[11]

This open interaction is imperative. Was the affair his reaction to your physical or emotional absence, or the evidence of a crisis in your own life? An escape from a dismal job situation or uncertainty about his masculinity? Was it an ego trip on his part, a support for feelings of inadequacy? Peer group pressure? Loss of self-esteem due to loss of a job or work problems? Fear of aging? Reduction of sexual capacities in marriage? Role or career change? Birth or sickness of a baby? Wife's leaving home for the work place? Revenge? Emotional dissatisfaction? A desperate cry for help? (Or any one of a hundred other considerations?) This is the kind of information you need to create understanding. You won't get all this insight in an hour; it may take days. And you certainly won't get it with nonaccepting criticism. But to ask, observe, and share, in order to become sensitive to the deeper meaning of the affair, is of utmost importance. The wife must put her cards on the table and convince her husband to do the same.

One warning. Do not probe for the juicy details. "Where did you two go when you were together?" "Were you thinking of her when you made love to me?" "Did you ever have her here in our house, in our bed?" One woman, learning her unfaithful husband used the Holiday Inn, exclaimed, "I'll never stay in a Holiday Inn again as long as I live!" There may be some details you are dying to know about, but don't ask them. They are irrelevant to resolving the problem. Knowing them may satisfy your curiosity and spark your jealousy but it will not contribute to the solution.

And resist every desire to ask questions that compare you in any way to the other woman, in looks, dress, performance.

Also, please, please don't ask him if he loves you. You force him into a double bind. At this point, he doesn't know; he's torn. He is living in the realm of his feelings and is undoubtedly deceived by those feelings. If you ask, "Do you still love me?" and he tells the truth, he might say, "No," or "I don't know," and then you would be shattered—hopeless. If he said, "Yes," you would be tempted to believe he is lying or to say, "Then why did you do such a thing? It proves you don't love me." This only aggravates the situation. At this point his actions speak more loudly than anything he can say.

INCREASE YOUR GROWTH, NOT YOUR GUILT

Perhaps the hardest thing of all to do—and at the same time the most necessary—is to examine the possibility of your own culpability in the affair. Have you in some way failed your partner? Dr. Mary Ann Bartusis, psychiatrist and author, points out what should be obvious to all: "It takes three corners to make a triangle, and one of these corners, inevitably, is yours."[12] Rarely does a husband or wife jump into a triangle until after the marriage is seriously ailing. The realization that we have failed in some way or contributed to the affair should not surprise us or throw us into a tizzy of self-defensiveness. After all, are you perfect? Do you make no mistakes? Are you not human like the rest of us, with limited understanding, personal weaknesses, sins, and possibilities of failure? Self-righteousness in any partner dooms the marriage at any stage. It's hard to live with perfection.

Why not swallow your pride and admit to yourself, to

God, and to your spouse what you really know to be true and face the hard and necessary question, "What have I done that contributed to the situation?" I am not suggesting a prolonged process of introspection, where you dissect all your faults, affirm how bad you are, and increase your guilt level. We don't need any more of that. Nor am I urging you to take all the blame for the whole mess, exonerating your partner of his sin. I have known women who were everything a husband could want, and still the husband cheated. There are more reasons for infidelity than an inadequate wife. But we do need to ask realistically, "Did I fail?" "What can I learn?" "How must I change?" Just as you expect your unfaithful partner to acknowledge his infidelity and learn from it, you must do the same with any failure on your part.

Redbook author Natalie Gittelson suggests this:

It behooves every wife who knows or suspects that her husband may be cheating to take a long fresh look at her own conduct, her own attitudes and her unspoken messages to the man in her life. She ought to ask herself frankly whether in certain subtle ways she may not be cheating him—of her time, sympathy, concern, compassion. Does she share her best ideas with her best friend and save for her husband only the drearier details of domesticity? Does she turn a deaf ear when he brings home some of the frustrations of his day and direct his attention instead to the frustrations of hers? Has he become low man on her totem pole of priorities? Scapegoat? Wailing wall? Problem child?[13]

One injured but now wiser woman agrees. "You can get awfully wound up in your kids and your job without meaning to and fail to give your husband the attention he needs. I found it wasn't better sex my husband wanted. He was looking for all the other kinds of attention I have been neglecting to give, even the occasional mothering that everybody needs at some time, that I sometimes want from him." Marjorie Zimmerman quotes one unfaithful but penitent husband, "A man has got to be more than a meal ticket in his own house."

An unnamed, saddened housewife adds her insight: "Looking back, I saw there had been many times—oh, so many times—when my husband reached out for closeness and understanding that I didn't give. I had always been doing something more pressing—like mending, cleaning the refrigerator or weeding the garden. I recalled the number of times he had said wistfully, 'Why don't we get off by ourselves for a couple of days? You can get a new dress maybe. And we can just loaf and be lazy—and young.' I hadn't said directly, 'Don't be silly; we're grownups,' but my lack of enthusiasm had doubtless been obvious." Another woman, though a strong Christian, gained another insight. "I'm so ashamed. I must have been a very dominating, self-righteous woman. And I never knew what I was doing."

Upon leaving his Christian wife, an unbelieving husband said candidly, "This girl isn't as pretty as you are—she isn't even very clean about herself. Without me she is an alcoholic. But she is the only person I know who ever needed me and accepted me just as I am. She has something for me you never had." Linda Wolfe adds, "Most adultery doesn't occur because of an individual's internal conflicts. Far more often, adultery is the result of an interpersonal conflict. A man's declining self-esteem may be involved but the wife herself may be the cause of that man's damaged ego. She may be overly critical or overly demanding of her husband or sexually unresponsive or even sexually rejecting."

A similar bit of counsel comes from Reformed Church pastor Henry Wildeboer:

Because the extramarital relationship often supplies what the marriage lacks, the answer is frequently one or more sins of

*omission, such as taking the other for granted, neglect, failing
to provide reassurance, negligence in expressing affection or
failure to be attractive, accessible, approachable. Sometimes
a spouse with a busy scheduled life appears disinterested or
cold. Children, clubs, business and church activities, important as they are, need to be kept in perspective. . . . When the
offended partner realizes his own shortcomings and their
contribution to the breakdown, he can with God's help begin
to forgive the offender and rebuild trust.*[14]

For Husbands Too

All that we have said goes for husbands, too, whose wives
have been unfaithful. Everything that a wife owes her husband, a husband owes his wife as well—without exception.
Best-selling author Dr. David Reuben notes, "A marriage is
like a long trip in a tiny rowboat: if one passenger starts to
rock the boat, the other has to steady it; otherwise, they will
go to the bottom together."[15]

"From my husband's affair," one woman told me, "I
learned so much about myself that I have become an entirely
different woman. I faced what I saw and heard about myself
and prayed that God would teach me, change me. I had a
deep experience with God, was really converted, and my
attitudes were changed. Over and over I prayed that God
would give me wisdom to become the most perfect mate
possible for my husband. Even my husband noticed it."

No marriage is rebuilt unless each partner is willing to learn
from the problem and make positive changes. No direct
action on my part will change my partner, but *I* can change.
God's grace is available to make me grow, to confess my sins,
my need, and He promises to "be faithful and righteous to
forgive my sins and cleanse me from all unrighteousness."[16]
He also promises to give me generously of His strength to do
what I cannot do alone.[17]

ALLOW EACH PARTNER
TO OWN HIS OWN ACTIONS

Since two people make up a marriage, if it fails, both bear some responsibility for its failure. Their responsibility is not alike, but they are alike responsible. One acts, the other reacts; one neglects the partner, the other neglects his vows. One is unfaithful in caring, the other unfaithful in adultery. No one can shoulder the other's burdens. Each must own his own action, regardless of what the other has done. Neither is responsible for the other's actions but each is responsible for his or her own behavior. "Whatsoever a man soweth that shall he also reap" applies to each one personally and particularly.

Shifting responsibility is a well practiced human trait begun by Adam. We like to play the "blame game" and look for a scapegoat. The unfaithful husband accuses, "You were so preoccupied with the kids that you never paid any attention to me," or, "Since you took that job I don't see you anymore," etc. He points the finger and says, "you," "you," "you." What *you* did excuses what *I* did. If he can get his wife to accept total responsibility, he can have his cake and eat it too. Like an alcoholic he can continue his destructive action, knowing his "mother" will protect him from the consequences and take all his guilt. Any woman who does this is only giving her husband practice in evasiveness and self-centered irresponsibility. Doctors Willard and Marguerite Beecher have a hard-hitting paragraph on this principle:

A person may have a problem or be one. The person who is a problem does not feel that he has one. He gets along splendidly exploiting and taking from others who put up with him. The person who puts up with him is the person who has the problem—the problem of providing support for the one who is the problem. In short, it takes both of them to make it possible for the one to fail![18]

I remember one man, Carl, who was a master at this. After being with his lover for a day or two he would come home and expect his wife to embrace him and make love with him. When she hesitated or refused he would say, "You are driving me right into the arms of this other woman. It will be your fault if our marriage breaks up. Is this what you want to happen?" He was a con man. The truth was, he had no intention of giving up his affair but wanted to keep the monkey on his wife's back. She was his garbage bag.

Any decision has to shift from blame to responsibility. Just as we *cannot* escape the part we played in the problem, we *dare not* excuse the part others play. We cannot defend the sin of adultery, but at the same time we can acknowledge our sin of neglect which contributed to the crisis. Some rejected wives, out of fear and insecurity, will assume all blame for their husbands' actions and will beg, plead, pressure, and accept any kind of abuse to keep them from leaving. "You can do anything, but don't leave me. What would I ever do without you?" No man in his heart respects that kind of woman. What she may think gives her control over him is really a sign of her weakness. She is saying, "I am not an important person." Her husband will leave her out of lack of respect or continue his affairs and stay to use her as a punching bag or a doormat.

Just as a straying husband voluntarily began his affair, he must voluntarily choose to stay in the marriage. Certainly you pray and trust God to bring about a change, but no amount of pressure will achieve this. You must open the cage so he is free to make a voluntary decision. Only this kind of choice is of any value in a marriage. At the same time, you convey the thought in the words of the Rev. Mr. Kreitler, "I think you'd be foolish to risk losing me," or "What we have together is too good to destroy." Years ago when we were discussing extramarital affairs and some friends we were trying to help, I asked my wife, Evelyn, "What would you do if you discovered I was involved in an affair and was determined to leave?" Without hesitation she answered, "I would be heartbroken and probably cry my eyes out. But God would help me through it and I would still have the memories of the good years we had together. But I wouldn't cry forever. There are a lot of men who would be thrilled to have a wife like me who would love them as I have loved you. And I am sure I wouldn't have any trouble finding one of them." A good answer. That's the kind of a wife you hold on to.

SHARE WITH A CONFIDANT
OR A COUNSELOR

According to medical authorities, 80 percent of all problems are self-healing. We should approach marriage problems the same way. "Yes," says Natalie Gittelson, whom I mentioned earlier, "the marriage that knits its own bones, so to speak, often is strengthened in the process. It is only when all else fails and an insoluble emotional emergency exists that psychological help from outside becomes essential."[19] So a couple should go as far as they can go in resolving the crisis unassisted by professionals.

However, sometimes the pain of infidelity is so great that the persons involved need to discharge their emotions to someone else before they can begin to be honest with each other. It's very hard to untangle the emotions of anger and guilt and get a fresh perspective. And they need to vent the emotions to someone who won't add fuel to the flames. This should probably be an unbiased third party, a minister, counselor, or family service agency. Forty to 50 percent of all the problems brought to today's minister have to do with marriage and family concerns. To seek needed counseling is a sign of strength, not weakness. It is the same as seeking a

specialist's expertise to save your eyesight rather than fool-
ishly and unnecessarily going blind.

I think it is wonderful that in our time the field of Christian
counselors is expanding rapidly, and in most metropolitan
centers there is a Christian counseling service. Many large
churches now have their own clinics. In seeking counseling,
first ask your pastor. If he feels he cannot help you, he can
recommend someone who can. If you are a Christian, do not
hesitate to ask a therapist about his spiritual values and his
objectives in counseling. Though others can help to some
degree, do everything possible to find a competent counselor
who appreciates your Christian commitment and can help
you within the framework of your faith, preferably one who
is successful in his own marriage and family. If his advice
hasn't worked for him it is of little help to you.

Anyone suffering the excruciating pain and loss from an
affair also needs a friend, a confidant—one who will listen,
but not talk. One who will support, but not sympathize—who
will give acceptance but not advice. Everyone has a host of
fringe friends who would enjoy sharing juicy morsels of
gossip or who always have the right advice for every situation
even though their own marriages are hardly vibrant. Avoid
these like the plague. Most people do not really understand
the complexities or ramifications of an affair and cannot give
objective counsel. They are quick to say "what I would do,"
or "I wouldn't trust him again," or "to thine own self be true."
These counselors are a dime a dozen. Don't syndicate your
sorrow. Instead, find a sounding board where you can open
your heart and calmly express your feelings and let your hair
down, a friend who will pray for you or pray with you—one
who doesn't have all the answers. A friend who, as the verse
says, "will take the chaff and grain together and with a breath
of kindness, blow the chaff away."

One such friend, or couple, is enough. Don't tell the

Sunday school class or the ladies' group, or the relatives. It is too tempting, in describing the problem, to run your partner down to gain sympathy. This then poisons the reputation of your husband once the affair is settled. There will be dark, dry spells, feelings of isolation. You will have a desire at times to hole up and avoid the embarrassment of seeing old friends or attending church alone. The minister and wife I mentioned in an earlier chapter, about whom Ellen Williams wrote, found strength in a church support group. The wife said, "The positive pressure of the Christian community was a big plus as we worked our way through this crisis. We had chosen to share our difficulty with one other Christian couple. They were able to support both of us. They became a holding pad for me as their steadying influence kept me hanging in when I might easily have blown it. In a symbolic way, they offered my husband acceptance and the assurance that nothing he had done could ever separate him either from the love of God or the church."

SEEK YOUR FORGIVENESS, THEN SPEAK YOUR FORGIVENESS

Whenever there is sin, a betrayal of trust, there is the matter of forgiveness. Whether it will be sought by the parties needing it or offered to the parties needing it, it goes without saying that an understanding of forgiveness is essential to a recovery from an affair. Forgiveness is the crucial issue. As anyone who has been through the experience will testify, restoring a marriage after infidelity is no easy matter. Forgiveness doesn't come quickly. It is costly. But it is the only way to healing and release, the only solution to deep pain.

What do we really know about forgiveness? How can it be practiced in such an emotion-charged situation?

Forgiveness Is Possible.
It is possible for both partners, the faithless and the injured. Adultery is not an unforgivable sin as some seem to think. The Bible does not catalog sin as though some sins are more heinous than others and some more easily forgiven. Some sins do more damage than others and are more far-reaching in their consequences. Paul talks about the uniqueness of adultery as it so seriously affects the body.

Flee immorality. Every other sin that a man commits is outside the body but the immoral man sins against his own body. Or do you not know that your body is the temple of the Holy Spirit who is in you, whom you have from God, and that you are not your own? For you have been bought with a price: therefore glorify God in your body.[20]

But every sin confessed can be forgiven. Nothing is impossible with God. After his affair with Bathsheba, David said: "I acknowledged my sin to thee and I did not hide mine iniquity; I said, 'I will confess my transgressions to the Lord'; then thou didst forgive the guilt of my sin."[21] Sins of omission within the marriage—neglect, rejection, self-centeredness, bitterness—can at times be far more corroding than adultery and must also be forgiven. Sins of the disposition must be confessed, as well as sins of the flesh. Every sin is primarily against God, though in an affair, many others are hurt—the partners on both sides, the two families, all the children. Since God created each of us, designed marriage and family relationships, and has a beautiful plan for each one, when we sin we are rejecting God's plan. God hates sin because it destroys the man He loves so much, so confession must be to Him first. David got this perspective: "Against thee, thee only, I have sinned and done that which is evil in thy sight."[22]

Forgiveness Is Necessary.

It is essential to our own mental health as well as to our marital health. David talked about the guilt and deception of his affair and how it drained him dry on the inside. And finally the release—"What relief for those who have confessed their sins and God has cleared their record. There was a time when I wouldn't admit what a sinner I was. But my dishonesty made me miserable and filled my days with frustration. All day and all night your hand was heavy on me. My strength evaporated like water on a sunny day until I finally admitted all my sins to you and stopped trying to hide them."[23]

Forgiveness Is Tough.

It strikes at the heart of our self-righteousness. Sometimes we enjoy feeling condemned. We cling to our hurts, still wanting to get even, to get revenge. To forgive is to let go of the hurt feelings, and that isn't easy. Our own self-hatred is often at the bottom of our unforgiveness; because we can't accept our own humanness, we are not free to accept our erring partner. Our inability to accept love limits our capacity to give it. We always judge others the way we judge ourselves. If we do not have a healthy self-love and see ourselves as valuable, growing people, often needing forgiveness, we cannot give our partner what we cannot give ourselves. Only when we see our own deficiencies are we ready to accept the imperfections of others. We cannot offer forgiveness out of a vacuum. As we receive and enjoy the love of God and of others, we learn to love.

We must let God love us. What we receive and experience, we can then share. The same is true of forgiveness. The more I am forgiven, the more forgiving I become.

Forgiveness Is a Choice.

Jesus puts forgiveness on the level of personal decision, not emotion. "And whenever you stand praying, *forgive,* if you have anything against anyone; so that your Father also who is in heaven may forgive you your transgressions."[24] This is a command, made to the will. Emotions, feelings, cannot be commanded. I must choose to forgive even when all my feelings cry against it. Often when I have struggled with forgiving someone, I've stood in my office and said audibly, loudly, "I forgive him, I forgive him, I forgive him." When I have set my will and heart in that direction, feelings of forgiveness follow and I can then say to the person involved, "I forgive you." It may take a while for all the hurt to leave but your choice releases the hold and time begins the healing process.

Forgiveness Is Not Forgetting.
Forgiveness is not an eraser that wipes the memory of the act forever from your mind. That's impossible. It is still history. The scar may be permanent. To forgive and forget is to forget the anger we feel toward the person who injured us—not to hold it against him and not to bring the skeleton out of the closet again. Even though we remember the deed, we treat the person as though it never happened. To constantly bring up the partner's affair in the bedroom or during other conflicts will ensure that the infidelity will never be forgotten by either one and it may encourage him to continue it.

Certainly where trust has been broken there may be questions for a period of time, occasional twinges of doubt, or echoes, but these will pass if there is a mutual effort to improve the marital relationship.

Forgiveness Is Offered.
I like the way Pastor Wildeboer expresses it:

As divine forgiveness depends not on man's feeling forgiven but on God's declaration of forgiveness, to be accepted on the basis of His word, so each partner must declare forgiveness of the other and accept the other's forgiveness on the basis of his word. Both parties will need to renew their commitment to each other, not only in an emotional way but with a declaration—and deeds to fit the words.... They will have to say to each other what, if they are Christians, they have already said to God: "I belong to you, heart, soul, mind and strength. I will do all I can to be faithful to you." Then they must practice loving each other. They must give as much of themselves as they are able to give—and want and work to give much more.[25]

This forgiveness can be the cornerstone of a stronger-than-ever marriage. Years ago I read a classic story of excellent forgiveness that moves me again as I write it. The woman kept it locked in her heart for half a century but shared it with "Dear Abby" to help others in the same position.

I was twenty and he was twenty-six. We had been married two years and I hadn't dreamed he could be unfaithful. The awful truth was brought home to me when a young widow from a neighboring farm came to tell me she was carrying my husband's child. My world collapsed. I wanted to die. I fought an urge to kill her. And him.

I knew that wasn't the answer. I prayed for strength and guidance. And it came. I knew I had to forgive this man, and I did. I forgave her, too. I calmly told my husband what I had learned and the three of us worked out a solution together. (What a frightened little creature she was!) The baby was born in my home. Everyone thought I had given birth and that my neighbor was "helping me." Actually it was the other way around. But the widow was spared humiliation (she had three other children), and the little boy was raised as my own. He never knew the truth.

Was this divine compensation for my own inability to bear

a child? I do not know. I have never mentioned this incident to my husband. It has been a closed chapter in our lives for fifty years. But I've read the love and gratitude in his eyes a thousand times.[26]

Anatomy of an Affair– and After!

A driving compulsion inside
fueled this torrid affair
for over two years.
Craving power,
he now had it over another person
and it was exhilarating.

HE amber-stuccoed building surrounded by acres of asphalt looked more like a warehouse than a church, a house of God. No white-columned pillars, cross-topped steeple, or finely manicured lawns. Parking spaces for hundreds of cars outside and simple chairs, not white and mahogany pews, inside, for the many hundreds of worshipers. In fact, a thousand in attendance on Sunday morning is quite common—more if the program is "special." This is the largest church in the county of this north central state.

On the church announcement board outside I noticed the schedule of services and one line in small script at the bottom which said, "Rev. Douglas Nelson, Pastor."* I wondered if those thousand worshipers knew the Doug Nelson story that I knew. The tragic past. The deception. The disaster. The affairs. How Doug and Sally had seen their marriage resurrected from the dead. Not long before, I had sat on their living room couch in their comfortable home and had probed with scores of questions. No question was rejected as too candid. No answer was withheld. I felt the pulse of their refreshingly open and transparent relationship, their deep understanding and commitment that have been shaped through some dark days and deep waters.

I was impressed that every principle I have mentioned in this book comes to life in their experience. They were willing to relive with me in graphic, moving detail every emotional moment "if it will help one other couple find their way back together." It is a true and illuminating story of power, passion, and beautiful promise.

Doug and Sally met each other at church during their

*Actual names and places have been changed, but the facts are true.

teens. Actually they didn't meet in a formal way since they had grown up together in the same church and attended the same high school, and had, in a way, always known each other. Coming from a home where both parents had known nothing but unbelievably hard work just to keep body and soul together, Sally was emotionally starved. Her parents certainly loved her—or they would protest they did—but didn't know how to express that love in ways that an insecure teenage girl could understand and receive. No affection was shown. It was work, work, work, interspersed with little more than eating, sleeping, and school. So, even as a high school sophomore, she had a tremendous need to be appreciated and loved. At this tender age when most girls were just hoping for a good grade in social studies or for a date to the class prom, Sally already had a strong desire for marriage and children. "Perhaps my thought of marriage was an escape from my tough home situation or a hope for relief from my poverty. But I know the first time I went with Doug that I wanted to marry him, that I *had* to marry him and that I would allow nothing to stand in the way of that."

Doug, a couple of years older, also became infatuated but the idea of early marriage scared him. He enjoyed the closeness but was far from ready to think of settling down. His parents, also not very affectionate, were successful, highly disciplined, and encouraged integrity, excellence, and a venturing ambition among their children. Church attendance was mandatory, good education a necessity.

Both Doug and Sally were active in the youth group and regularly attended the annual church revival meetings. But there was no one to talk to; at least they didn't think so. No one with whom they could share their struggles and fears. And like many teens whose parents have not been affectionate with them, their emotions were on the surface waiting to be ignited by a word, a touch, and another warm body. If a girl has grown up being touched and held in a wholesome way by her father, the most important man in her life, she will be less vulnerable sexually to the first boy that holds her hand.

"We both enjoyed being close," recalls Doug. "And before we knew it, we had developed a sexual intimacy that lasted all the way through college, on and off. It was always there and we would battle it constantly. We had this secret for years and no one knew." When I asked about their relationship to the church, he continued. "We were both Christians and church members so we would immediately repent, abstain for a while, then yield again to the temptation. We had no inner supports. We knew all of the ethics—the Ten Commandments, the 'oughts,' but that was not enough to keep us out of bed. An occasional sermon against immorality only seemed to drive us deeper into self-condemnation and guilt. There was no help on the outside; not that it was withheld, it just wasn't there. None of the adults seemed to be aware of the struggles we were having. Perhaps they had forgotten their own past or had gone through their teen-age years with their glands out of gear."

Marriage came the week following graduation and a few weeks later Doug entered an evangelical seminary in New York. The marriage was the culmination of four years of engagement and a beautiful dream for Sally. But it was a decision of duty for Doug. "I began to realize I was marrying her because of a deep sense of honor placed in my life by my parents. I knew that I had somehow dishonored this woman, deflowered her, and that I should marry her. Though I was infatuated with her, we entered marriage with that understanding and it was never a very deep experience with me at all. However, we were a fun couple and did a lot of fun things together."

Sally adds, "But it was a great in-love feeling for me which had continued from high school. I had my infatuation and love all tied together in one package and was thrilled to be Doug's wife and was looking forward to having children."

At seminary the pace did not slacken. Night-time jobs to support the family, two children to care for, and much religious activity. Though Doug was studying to be a minister and deeply involved in church affairs, Sunday school classes, seminary activities . . . "there was no sense of the intimacy of Christ in me—of the Holy Spirit actually functioning inside of my life." When I asked if he were aware of this spiritual vacuum, he exclaimed, "Oh, my no! Everybody else was doing the same so we were all caught up in good Christian service. In fact, had you asked me then, I'm sure that I would have said that I was fulfilled in every way. But what we thought was a cloud of God's anointing over us was probably nothing more than the dust of our own activity."

Their marriage at this point was typical of most school couples. They huddled together and clung a lot, struggling to find their own way. Neither set of parents had modeled a demonstrative affectionate relationship. They were learning from each other and they both agreed it was "difficult." Sally said she had great emotional needs, was deeply jealous, and clung to Doug for security. Both of them were at a shallow spiritual level. A shell had formed around them, the shell of their early times together, and "we survived on the physical experience of love, the thrill of children, the excitement of going into the ministry."

"But though our marriage then was quite ordinary," Doug recalls, "my own ambitions were anything but dormant. Growing in me was a driving desire for success and power. My only goal was to climb to the top of the ecclesiastical ladder, become pastor of the largest church in the country and also become the president of our large denomination. That would have been the epitome of success to me."

Everything seemed to fall in place. It seemed God was

smiling on them and following their plan. Their first invitation right out of seminary was to a very large church as associate pastor. Hardly had their furniture been arranged in the parsonage when tragedy struck—not to them, but to the senior pastor. A critical heart attack and he was removed, incapacitated. Only one month had gone by and now this aggressive seminary grad was catapulted into the senior pastor's position at the age of twenty-six.

Sitting behind the senior pastor's desk was a heady thing for this young preacher. He had power, prominence, and control; people were converted, the church grew, but he was like a new sailor at the helm of a battleship. When asked if he was capable of doing the job, he confidently repeated the spiritual-sounding cliché, "God and I can do anything together." But it was a hollow boast from a hollow man. Flushed with the feeling that he was on the road to success, he began maneuvering his way through the channels of influence and power in the community. While he was enjoying the exhilarating company of the town's business and professional leaders in the YMCA, Rotary, Lions, and Kiwanis, his marriage was held together only by the whirling activity around them. "I was power-hungry. I wanted to be king. I wanted to be president of every organization." Sally was wrapped up in the children—another one had come—and didn't understand Doug's need to be praised or his struggle with a growing inner emptiness. His words are graphic. "The gnawing for love which was deep inside of me had been almost cannibalistic—seeking to devour any around me who seemed willing to be consumed." Sally didn't grasp this. Instead of drawing together for support and understanding with a focus on their marriage, each had his or her own project—his church, her children. Their personal needs unrecognized, unmet. A vacuum. A perfect setting for an affair.

Even for a minister.

And no surprise. Ministers are no less susceptible to the surging drive of sex and passion than anyone else. If anything, they're more susceptible. They're exposed to every kind of emotional and spiritual sickness. Those who come for help are reaching out for love and empathy. Someone to care. Any minister with just a touch of compassion cannot help but identify and feel with his people who hurt. Not only ministers but anyone in a helping profession faces the same temptations. One minister told me years ago how his counseling of a young woman at his prayer altar became his downfall. As she was wiping away tears of joy, he comforted and embraced her. Two warm bodies touched and melted together. The fuse was lit. Soon came the inevitable explosion.

That's how Doug's first affair started. An innocent kiss from a thankful girl in gratitude for God's working in her life. Her motive was pure but a fuse was lit that was part of a chain reaction, and though she and her young minister were both innocent . . . well, let's hear Doug tell it.

"The thought of immorality with any of the ladies in my church had never entered my mind. I thought I was beyond that. Then one night I baptized a young woman who had been a real streetwalker but had now come to Christ. After that evening baptismal service, she dressed and came back into my study to thank me. Her hair was still wet from the service. To my surprise she threw her arms around me and kissed me smack on the mouth and said, 'You don't know how wonderful and clean I feel now.' That was probably a very natural kind of expression for her—very mild. It was all so spontaneous and, I'm sure, pure. No hidden agendas on her part, but bells started ringing inside me and it opened up all kinds of hungers. The memory of that kiss lingered with me for days. I relished and rehearsed it and began to feel that I was on the verge of a new adventure—not looking for something, but certainly open to it."

That satanic trap had been laid and he had smelled the bait. It was already too late to follow the advice of John Dryden, "Better shun the bait than struggle in the snare." And one month later, opportunity arrived to meet desire. If one is waiting at the door of temptation, the devil will see to it that someone is there to kick it open. And that open door always seems so natural, so compatible, so predestined.

It was four o'clock in the afternoon when the door swung wide open, opened by a "good friend." "I remember vividly walking into a hospital room to visit the wife of a family who were our best friends. We lived just a few blocks apart, had taken some vacations together, were active in the same church, and the wife was an especially close friend to Sally. They did many things together and thought highly of each other. As I was getting ready to leave, she reached out to hold my hand and said, 'You don't know this, but I've had this inside of me for two years. I'm deeply in love with you. I love you with all my heart.' Wow! Like the Fourth of July. Everything started exploding inside and all around me. My heart began to pound and my palms got sweaty and my mouth began to get dry, my eyes dilated. But I savored those first embarrassing feelings and walked out of the hospital on air. The rest of the afternoon was a blur and I was back at seven o'clock to hear her say it again. At nine the next morning I returned to hear it again and to kiss and embrace. We both began to live for the day when she was to be released and we could 'show our love for each other.'"

That pastoral visit became a passionate calling that could not be denied. A driving compulsion inside fueled this torrid affair for over two years. For two years they had their secret signals in church, their secret places for love notes, their secret rendezvous. Craving power, he now had it over another person and it was exhilarating. "And I began to experience the same feelings I had had in high school when Sally and I first began our little intimacies. Those heart palpitations now returned again and I said to myself, 'I am in love.'"

At this point I felt I needed to ask, "Sally, where were you? What was happening back at the range?" Sally picked up the story. "Well, I knew something was wrong immediately but was not sure what it was. I suspected there was something between Doug and Joanne but I didn't know how far it had gone or how to fight it. My intuitions were picking up signals all over the place and flashing red lights. I tried to back off from Joanne's family—no more dinners together, no more socializing, no more vacations—but Doug insisted we keep them as friends.

"But there was one good thing," Sally continued. "This situation knocked Doug right off the pedestal I had him on. I had thought he could do no wrong—a man of God. I was really trusting him more than I was trusting God. So, this problem really pushed me back on God and my relationship with Christ began to deepen and He became more real to me."

For two years things continued but not as they had been before. That was impossible. Something had to give. What goes on behind the closed doors of the preacher's heart and mind as he becomes mesmerized by his "stolen apples" and galvanized by his deception? How does a man ride three wild horses at once and retain his balance when they're all going in different directions? Their names? Marriage, ministry, mistress. The Chinese have a proverb: "He who sacrifices his conscience to ambition burns a picture to obtain the ashes." What was happening to this threefold picture as the flame of passions and power continued uncontrolled? How does a man retain his sanity when these forces of his inner hell converge?

By this time the marriage was in trouble. Sally knew for sure Doug was sleeping with her friend and there were daily confrontations. Accusations. Threats. "In public, when rumors of the affair began to leak out, I defended Doug. I wasn't about to allow others to throw stones at him. I felt it was something we had to discuss behind closed doors. I even denied the fact to the church people while I was confronting him constantly about it in private. We beat each other up. Sometimes it got physical when I threatened to expose him, to leave. The children became my weapons against him, and to get his attention I would say to them in his presence, 'If you knew about your daddy,' or 'Your daddy is. . . .' But he only became more infuriated. My attitude was raunchy but I was just lashing out in pain any way I could.

"Furthermore, I was always questioning his salvation. I didn't understand how he could be involved with somebody else and still have a relationship with God. And there was no one I could turn to. Many times I felt that I was carrying this load all alone. I felt humiliated, wounded, rejected. But there was never a thought or threat of divorce. We'd sealed that when we entered marriage, so I never gave up. Certainly Doug was letting God down, letting me down, but I knew God would bring him to his senses even though it was painful and hurtful. I believed with all my heart that as long as I stayed obedient to God, He would take care of my husband.

"And you probably wonder about our sex life. Though I used everything else against him, I never withheld sex. Sexually, I tried to meet all of his needs and that was a 'biggy.' I realized he was going elsewhere to get satisfied and I kept thinking if he were satisfied at home he'd cut it off elsewhere. Lots of times I had to grit my teeth but I knew I would be wrong if I withheld it. To add my wrong to his wrong wouldn't help. Two wrongs don't make a right."

What was Doug's reaction to this? "Sally's right. Though

she knew I'd been with a woman that morning, she never withheld sex that night. I think had she done that, she would have driven me out of the house. But she said this was my problem, not hers, and she was here to give herself to me. Everything I have, I owe to her."

But what was happening to Doug's conscience? "Of course, any man who commits adultery also lies. They exist side by side. In the lying the progression began very rapidly. I had to manipulate her, overpower her. To Sally's accusations I would say, 'You're imagining things. There's something wrong with you. Normal people aren't jealous like this.' I tried to convince her she was emotionally unbalanced. That she was really insane.

"And there was this terrible conflict inside. I felt that I loved them both. I would dream sometimes at night. What if I had to make a choice? They're both in the car, the car is on fire, and I can only get one of them out. Which one would I take out? If only my wife would die! Though I didn't express it verbally, this death wish became so strong that it was spiritually transferred over to Sally. And she began to want herself dead. I literally put it on her in the spirit. Intuitively. Sin always ends in death, either in actuality or in purpose. It starts out as a flirty little thing but winds up with you really wanting your wife dead."

What about Doug's ministry? Did he have a problem with sinning on Saturday night and preaching the gospel on Sunday morning? Another pastor I know became more legalistic and judgmental in his preaching to turn attention away from his own sins. Doug responded. "I became hardened. It was a driving obsession inside of me to keep this affair going regardless, and I never stopped to analyze the crazy, stupid things I was doing. There was no weekly struggle before going into the pulpit, wondering how could I do this. I was totally blind. There was so much blindness and deception that I could justify what I was doing. In fact, I would preach better if I had been with Joanne on Saturday night. But I hedged my preaching. I would not call adultery sin from the pulpit. I'd ease around it. I would be very careful about attacking the liar. It would sound right but I would come right up to the edge and back off, lest I condemn myself in the process. But no one could ever say I was not scriptural.

"And people were being saved. Marriages being healed. I am still mystified at this because my theological background said that God can't use people like that. And my logic says there's no way to put those two things together. But I was like those stone lions that have water coming out of their mouths. The power of the Lord was working through me but He wasn't working in me."

But God's time finally came, at least the beginning of it. His strategy with each person is different but the principles are the same. One by one, he removes the supports and strips us bare, until He can get our attention. Sometimes it is an overpowering direct approach. At other times, an inner leanness develops. But He is determined to complete the work He begins in us no matter how many obstacles our pride puts in the way. He will get us back on the main line regardless of all the rabbits we've been chasing. In His own way and at His own time, He dispatches the hounds of heaven.

With Doug it started during the Christmas and New Year holidays. He had sent the family off to relatives in Michigan and decided to spend the better part of the week by himself in the parsonage. "On New Year's Eve I remember sitting home alone, no one else in the house, and getting down beside a chair and beginning to cry. And not knowing why. I had never had an emotional explosion like this. I suddenly realized that I was reamed out from the inside and I hadn't sensed it. I didn't know how to pray anymore. I remember sitting there trying to pray about Sally, the children, and Joanne, and nothing came out. God was gone. It was the first experience I had of my extreme spiritual emptiness. The only thing I could do was just weep and sob and say, 'What's wrong with me?' and 'Oh, God help me.' I was not specifically going to say, 'Remove me from this.' I could not ask that. All I could say was 'Help me.'

"Within the next month, I realized that everything was falling to pieces inside of me. In fact, I began to wonder if I could continue in the ministry. Conviction began to build— deep conviction that I was a fraud and that the situation was deteriorating around me. My girl friend was beginning to make unusual demands on me that I could not fulfill. She would call me on the phone, wanting to know if I had had sex with my wife the night before. I couldn't handle that. Extreme jealousy. She wanted everything from me, which, of course, is a woman's natural bent. I could handle a wife and a mistress but I couldn't handle two wives. That was far beyond me and I was being crushed in the middle of it.

"The next Sunday morning was church. I went over early, about 7:30, to go over my sermon and get ready for the services. As I stepped inside I heard the organ and sat in the back row. Our organist, a single girl of about twenty-seven, was practicing her music for the morning worship. There was no one else in the building. As I listened to the music, I began to weep again uncontrollably. When I got up and walked down the aisle, she noticed that I was really distraught and said to me, 'What can I do? I know something's wrong.' Suddenly I realized that she knew that I was falling apart and probably knew the reason. I began to sense that probably a lot of other people did, too.

"She came back into my study with me and before I knew it I kind of vomited out to her what I had not said to anyone else. I sobbed. 'This thing with Joanne is killing me.' 'Yes, I know,' she answered sympathetically. Suddenly I found myself in her arms and she was soothing and caressing me and saying, 'I understand.' And from that moment on, the affair with Joanne was over. That finished it. I never went back to her. I felt in my mind that I had been released from that and I transferred everything to the organist. Just picked it up here and set it down right over there. Affair number two."

"Jealousy is the injured lover's hell," wrote John Milton— "and cruel as the grave," adds Solomon. Joanne, now jilted, decided if she couldn't have the pastor, no other woman would. Sally's phone began to ring off the wall. Anonymous calls several times a day. "Who's your husband having intercourse with tonight?" The children got calls from a disguised woman's voice saying, "Do you know who your daddy is sleeping with?"

In my interview with Doug, now a mature man of God, I noticed several times that he flinched almost in disbelief that he could have been so utterly stupid and foolish. I couldn't help but question. "What were the elements of these affairs? What did you think these women provided for you that your wife didn't provide at home? Laughter, surprises, gifts, appreciation, building up your ego?"

"Allan, I don't know. I've looked at that. My wife loved me dearly and of course, these two women said they did too. I think it was the thrill of the different."

"Like stolen apples?"

"Yes, I'm sure it was stolen apples. The greener grass. The forbidden thing. I used to go behind the house and smoke when I was a kid because my parents wouldn't allow me to smoke otherwise. And I would have felt it wrong to smoke in their presence. My godly parents set very high standards for me. That's why I never considered divorce. I could lie, cheat, commit adultery, but I couldn't get a divorce because divorce is ungodly.

"My moral ethical structure was a superstructure. It was not built within—it was built without, so I was constantly trying to fight my way out of this prison. It wasn't until much later that the morality became a part of me on the inside."

But Joanne's jealous efforts were beginning to pay off. Her accusations were being made more and more public until there was a growing pressure of people beginning to say that the pastor and the organist were having an affair. But nobody could prove anything. Yet.

Confidently but stupidly, Doug was carrying on with this girl the way he had with Joanne. Same kind of love notes, in the same places. But one "I love you" note left on the organ keyboard never made it to the organist. It ended up in the hands of a deacon. Black and white evidence. The hounds of heaven had flushed out their fugitive.

The deacons demanded an immediate resignation. Unable to manipulate the political structure of the church any longer, Doug was trapped. Twice before, he had bluffed his way through church business meetings and gotten a vote of confidence. To leave voluntarily would have meant an admission of guilt. It would also mean leaving behind a relationship in which he reveled with the same degree of intensity as an alcoholic does his bottle. Now he was laid bare. His insides were churning. Desperately he tried to hold the facade of false confidence. But it started to crack when he was asked to leave the meeting and wait outside as they discussed the matter.

"Instead of at least a pretense of a sedate exit, I bolted. Fled. I stumbled into the darkened sanctuary and knelt at the front, weeping in fear and confusion. Back in the conference room the men were deciding my fate. In the next room was a small office. I called Sally. 'Come get me. I can't take it anymore.' I hung up and in a state of nearly choking shame, faced with the awfulness of it all, I wandered down a flight of stairs lit only dimly by the quiet red exit light.

"She found me, the shepherd of the flock, crouched in a fetal position in a basement hallway, huddled against the landing of the stairs. 'It would be better for you, for the children, for this church if I were dead,' I sobbed.

"She comforted. She soothed. She never asked for details. There was no need. She led me by the hand through the dark hallways of the house of God to our car parked under the lighted window of the conference room. I did not realize it at the time, but those men were God's servants—sent by the Holy Spirit to perform the unpleasant task of shaking a man of God until only the unshakable remained.

"That night I walked into the front yard of our beautiful parsonage. Standing under the autumn sky, I looked up into the heavens and screamed: 'Take me! Take me now! Quickly!' In a desperate move, I grabbed my shirt and ripped it open at the chest, tearing the buttons and hem as I exposed my bare chest to the heavens, waiting for the flash of lightning which I expected to come and split me asunder, carrying me into the hell where I belonged.

"But there was no flash of lightning, for the purging fire had already begun to burn. And besides, God does not punish sin the way we punish it. As ranchers often burn off a pasture to kill the weeds so the new grass can sprout, so the consuming fire of God burns away the dross without consuming the sinner."

The exposure and resignation followed. The church gave them three months' salary, three months in the parsonage, but only until Friday to clean out the pastor's study with the clear warning that they were never again welcome in that church building at any time. The church leaders hardly knew how to handle this situation. Throughout the entire state and region, the grapevine had quickly carried the sad news to denominational pastors and leaders.

Doug desperately reached out for his friends, only to find

they had all departed. He was unclean, a leper. Ninety-two letters were written to influential friends saying, "I'm without a church. I need help." Only one even bothered to reply. Maybe these men knew what God knew—and probably Doug, too—that he wasn't ready for another church. For in spite of the brokenness, rejection, and failure, he was really no different on the inside. Only the outside label had been changed on an empty bottle. He was still the magnificent manipulator, the master of control, the defender of his position. He was still pushing people around, still more of a politician than a man of God.

A small but growing church opened up in Ohio—the only one available. But in order to get the church Doug lied about his reason for resignation. After moving, Sally huddled with the five children at home while Doug continued his contacts with the organist, now in another state, who had been fired simultaneously with him. There were correspondence, phone calls, the private post office box, clandestine meetings. Out-of-town trips made on church business always included a secret stopover, but it was no secret to Sally. She had become quite a detective finding the calls on the telephone bills, revealing notes, motel receipts. "Every time he would leave to go on a trip," Sally remembers, "I knew he was going to see her. I could even tell it in the way he acted. Often I told him I could take the truth better than I could take his lies. I'd find it out anyway and that was more hurtful than if he had just told me the truth to begin with."

Soon echoes from the past began drifting to Ohio—rumors of adultery, of manipulation, of lying. And Doug's feelings? "I continued to fight, to brave the growing onslaught of fact that kept building up against me. The old undertow sucked at my guts and I felt I was about to be swept back to sea.

"The crisis exploded one Sunday morning when I stepped up to the pulpit to preach. On the pulpit stand was a petition asking me to resign. It was signed by 350 people, many of whom were sitting smiling in the congregation. A group of men had hired a private detective and checked into my past. The detective's report—all forty-seven pages of badly distorted facts—had been duplicated and handed out to the congregation. The deacons demanded I take a lie detector test. Even though I passed it, it was not enough. I was fired. I had no choice but once again to slink home and huddle with my wife and children while the fire of God continued its purging work."

There was a small group of people who left the church with him, still believing in him, and they met as a struggling little congregation in a store front.

Stripped of everything he had walked over so many people to get—power, control, recognition—Doug now had time to think. At thirty-five years of age, he was a broken man with broken dreams and years of failure behind and around him. For months he had been floating with the tide, buffeted by whatever circumstances came along. Empty, purposeless, but still somehow determined to make his own way.

But the beginning of a one hundred and eighty degree change was a "chance" meeting with a stranger who had become his friend. This friend had shared a deep spiritual experience—some of the great things God had done for him—and had invited Doug to attend a conference with him in Chicago. Conferences were old hat to this pastor, but this was to be the trip of a lifetime. All his other rendezvous during the last several years he had arranged himself and pursued relentlessly. This one was prepared by God. Doug had no idea what awaited him, his family, and his future when he walked through that hotel lobby to the ballroom where the conference was being held.

Being a visitor with no particular responsibilities at this gathering, Doug observed the people as they poured into the meetings. He sensed their delight and excitement at just being there. There were meetings with different speakers all day long for various groups—a smorgasbord of spiritual opportunities for teaching, inspiration, and fellowship. Personal contacts between the meetings, over the dinner table, and in the halls brought Doug face to face with people whose lives had been radically and beautifully changed by God. All of this began to focus on an inner emptiness at the center of Doug's being that had been ringed by his religious upbringing, training, and activities. This sense of hollowness only increased his struggle as he sat in the final evening gathering. With no thought of getting personally involved or responding to the public appeal of the speaker to come to the front for prayer, he put his head on the back of the seat in front of him.

Suddenly, without warning, he began to cry uncontrollably—crying so hard he could hardly catch his breath. It was as if all the dams inside had burst and he was being flooded from within. He felt the arm of a friend around him and heard his voice praying for him. Up to this time, Doug had always been concerned about public opinion, his public image. Previously, tears were in private. No one had known or had seen them. Now he was sobbing convulsively with people all around him. Laid bare. No longer able to control or manipulate his emotions to his own ends.

The intense emotional turmoil revolved around the one point of his whole life conflict—a fear. "I knew that if I turned loose, God would take all the things I held precious, leaving me helpless, totally dependent on Him. But I could struggle no longer and, like a wild mustang, was totally broken to my new owner—God Himself. A great peace swept over me as though God had taken His hand and wiped away the tears. For the first time in my life I felt I was a 'whole person.' The lights had been turned on in my black pit.

"When I got back to my hotel room it was midnight. The

first thing I wanted to do was to call Sally, wake her up and tell her. I said, 'I just need to call you and tell you I deeply love you.' And I wept again. A different kind of tears this time. Clean. Refreshing."

What was Sally's reaction to Doug's call and what significance did it have? Undoubtedly she thought he was visiting his girl friend as well as attending a conference. "Yes, but when he called weeping at midnight to tell me he loved me, I knew that something had broken inside. He had never shown emotions such as crying before—at least not in my presence. Then, of course, I began to cry, too. He couldn't even explain what had happened to him but the rest of that wonderful sleepless night I wondered if this was finally the answer to my prayers."

The next day Doug flew straight home, with a new gripping desire this time—to tell Sally the whole story—all about his encounter with God and all about his two affairs. As they lay together in bed, he began a confessional that lasted most of that Sunday night. "I opened my life to everything I had done, everything I was doing and everything I had planned to do for the next few days—because I had a rendezvous set up for the following day in another city. I laid it all out. The lies, the deception. Though she cried, she handled it extremely well. She never demanded details though I was prepared to give her every detail, anything she asked. It was a great catharsis, though very painful for Sally and especially painful for me.

"For the first time in my life, however, I realized that if our lives and marriage could be saved, it would have to be through honesty. The only way I could do that was to disarm myself and give her the firing pin of the grenade and say, 'You hold it. You can blow me up at any time if you want to but you need to know everything about me.' There was an act of my will that I would never again let anything come into our relationship that I could not share with her. Anything."

Forgiveness! The word is beautiful and comes easy. But how do you forget years of deceit and devastation? This was Sally's problem. Doug's confession was like the rising of the sun after seven years of night. How do you become accustomed to the light when that light begins to reveal something about you? Is forgiveness over in a moment but the healing takes longer? Does forgiving automatically restore trust? What about scars?

I turned to Sally seated in a chair next to me and noticed the peace and serenity etched in her face. She was a delightful woman, now in her late forties. "Of course, I was overjoyed," she mused thoughtfully. "But I was a bit frightened at the same time. Would it last? I had been disappointed so many times before that I hesitated to let myself totally believe that all the nightmare was over. I couldn't fully relax. As time went by, God began to reveal to me my self-righteous attitudes. I was still critically judging my husband and feeling sorry for myself, and I reached out to possess him, to control him. If I could just hold onto him, not let him out of my clutches, he couldn't go wrong anymore. That possessiveness also caused me to try to change him so we wouldn't have any more trouble. I finally saw that if God had started this new work in Doug, only God could continue and complete it. So, with all my will I relinquished him totally to God—turned him loose. 'He's yours. . . . He really doesn't belong to me.' And that is when the real healing started to come about."

Across the room I looked at Doug—hardly a picture now of the man he had described to me. A few pounds overweight, as I am, he has a pleasant face with a ready smile, animated features, a quick mind. "What was the bottom line?" I asked. "What really came out of that cleansing and healing experience with God? Certainly it affected your emotions, but how did it change your attitude, your actions?"

His answer was crisp, clean. "I was moved toward truth—truth with my wife, truth with God. Immediately after that experience I determined that I would spend the rest of my life being honest. I knew what being deceitful cost us. Forgive the expression, but we both had had the hell beat out of us. So being honest hasn't really cost us anything. Also a new appreciation for my wife began to develop. I saw her in a new light. I not only discovered she was equal with me in her relationship with God, and in her intelligence and emotional makeup, but in many areas she excels far beyond what I do. She hears God sometimes much better than I do. In many areas she's smarter than I am. I also noticed that I wanted to put my arm around her in public and hold her hand, which was not my normal practice.

"One other thing. I began to see the difference between love and infatuation. The feelings that come from infatuation I cannot control. But I can control how I will express those feelings in action. I can control whom I call on the telephone. Whom I write. I can control whom I go to see, when I go to see this person, and whom I go with. I learned that love is an act and that I would have to begin working at it—that my feelings are to be brought under control of my acts."

It has been fifteen years now since Doug and Sally's marriage came back from the dead. Their spacious home has become a Bethel—a house of God where they now have a far-reaching ministry to other fractured couples who are struggling with their pain of an affair. They have endured the pain themselves. They can understand, empathize. They have been through the crucible of suffering caused by their self-inflicted wounds. They can now warn with compassion and certainty. If even one couple can discover through them that there is hope and healing, they feel that their experience will not have been in vain.

As they both talked with such candor and openness about

their failures and restoration my heart was warmed and encouraged. I wished that other troubled couples I have known could have confronted their problems so successfully. I arose from the comfortable couch and prepared to leave. The youngest daughter came in—a lovely nineteen-year-old. A little grandson in diapers peeked around the corner. Other grandchildren living nearby played in the back yard. It was a tranquil scene. I hated to leave but my plane would not wait.

But I had one more question for each of them. "What deep lessons have been branded into your souls from all this and how do you handle the echoes of the past?"

Sally spoke first. "First a word about forgiveness. It is easy to forgive someone when you really love him. That is the only reason I could keep on forgiving Doug during all those years. Forgiveness is not just something you do. It is something you are. It is not words that come out of my mouth saying, 'I forgive you.' It is the way a person lives. It is not putting off retaliation to a better time. It is wiping the slate clean.

"Also, divorce was never an option. In looking back, I'm thankful that no one came along and counseled me to get a divorce. If I had been abused physically, separation or divorce might have been necessary for my protection. I know I had every legal and moral right to divorce, but I chose to stay. I see the whole message of the cross calling us to stay in the marriage relationship and die to self there. How else is new life going to spring up in your mate unless you're willing to 'die'?

"Finally, healing doesn't happen overnight. But it always starts with truthfulness—as painful as that may be. It takes a long time but it gets better all the time. The scars are still there but time is the healing factor. I focus on the happy experiences of our recent years instead of the bad memories of the dark past. When an echo of the past reappears we can now face it together with openness. Because I believe marriage is forever,

God enabled me to hang in there and now He has blessed us beyond our imagination."

Doug concluded. "I'm convinced that a mystical union in marriage is a reality. We have become one. We're no longer two people living in the same house, two bodies sleeping in the same bed. Something has happened in our spirits which has made us one. This oneness of marriage necessitates that each partner have total access to everything going on in the mate. That does not mean dredging up the past and revealing everything that happened before marriage. But it does mean living in openness now in our relationship. I counsel couples in the way I wish someone had taught us when we started out. Make a covenant together that no matter how it hurts, you will share every feeling you have with your mate. Not facts alone, but feelings as well, because feelings are the things that always lead us into fact. We are not really responsible for our feelings but for how we express and act them out.

"Sally and I have deliberately worked at this concept of truth. The thing that will destroy the marriage is the lie. Adultery alone does not necessarily destroy the marriage; it is the lie. We were able to handle the adultery when we brought it into the light. Every man has flaws and sins. It is only when you keep it in the darkness that sin grows and multiplies. If it is brought into the light, then there is help for it. Before, I would not bring it into the light because I didn't want help. Now I want help. So if I'm tempted and sin, I want to get it exposed immediately and that means I must include my wife. We also belong to a covenant group with four other couples where we share and support each other.

"Also, remember that insight that was mentioned briefly before regarding love and trust. My wife saw this before I did because she found it so hard to trust me. We're really not called to trust one another. There's no one I can totally trust. Everybody is capable of letting me down or betraying me, and I am capable of betraying other people. We're called to trust the One who will never betray us, never let us down. But we're called to love one another. If our relationship is based on trust, then the moment that trust is broken the relationship is broken. So I trust God and love my wife. She trusts God and loves me. And if she lets me down, I'm going to continue to love her anyway because that is my commitment. Sally's love kept reaching out to me and closing the gap that I was constantly creating by my adultery. She was always coming out to meet me. The distance between us remained the same because she kept initiating love. Her uncondemning love is the thing that has covered a multitude of sins.

"Let me also add to Sally's word about forgiveness. We tend to want instant forgiveness from each other. Only God can provide that. When I tell my wife it's over, I want her never to bring it up again because I think she should be like God—it is wiped forever from her memory. But she's not like God. She operates in the area of time while God operates in timelessness. We've discovered that time and patience are required for forgiveness to mature in each of us so we often have to wait for each other while it develops.

"Finally, I know that failure is neither fatal nor final. God is a restoring God who picks us up where we are and gives us a new beginning. I have been in the cesspool. I can tell you exactly where it is, what it smells like, and what comes out of it. I know what affairs do to your partner and your children if you pursue this course. But Sally and I stand as a testimony that regardless of how dark any marriage situation is right now, or how much of a cloud may hang over you because of past failure, God can forgive completely. The fields that have been eaten by the grasshoppers are restored with beautiful crops."

In those dark circumstances I don't know of anything better than that assurance.

CHAPTER 9

Affair-Proof
Your Marriage

There is no better safeguard

against infidelity

than a vital,

interesting marriage.

Dr. Norman M. Lobenz

N A TRIP to Alaska, Evelyn and I were provided a one-week expense-paid vacation in the fabulous Mount McKinley National Park. We were flown into the park by small plane over deep mountain chasms and beautiful lakes and between magnificent peaks. Breathtaking scenery! We transferred to a sightseeing bus for the five-hour trip back through mountains to the remote Camp Denali with our congenial host, Wally Cole.

Like kids on their first trip to Disneyland, we were all oh's and ah's and eyes. It was a photographer's paradise. Grizzlies, caribou, moose, dall sheep, rare birds—we saw them all. And the highest peak in North America, Mount McKinley, was spectacular, awesome, majestic, overwhelming!

But on this forever memorable journey there were also many ordinary signs along the road—warning signs: *Beware of Falling Rock. Do Not Leave the Road. Camping at Your Own Risk.* Also helpful signs: *Scenic Rest Stops. Scientific Station. Historical Monuments.*

Marriage is like that—a long and memorable journey. And it becomes more meaningful when you pay close attention to the signs. And more safe—safe from an extramarital affair. First, the warning signs.

DON'T COMPARE THE INCOMPARABLE

No two marriages are in any way alike. Therefore, to compare them is a negative exercise, breeding negative results. If you compare your marriage to the many around you that are collapsing in a pile or are only endurance contests, you will become discouraged, feel out of sync with the times. Or you will become complacent, thinking you have nothing to worry about. If you focus on marriages you think really have it made, you fall short, magnify your own inabilities, and despair. You can never meet the standard.

The truth is, there is no standard marriage. Comparisons are like a revolving door that gets you nowhere. You go round and round and then end up in the same place. You only confirm your conviction that you have a second-class marriage or increase your fear that you will fail in a first-class one. Both of these attitudes kill personal initiative which is necessary to a successful marriage. No wonder the Bible says, "Those that compare themselves among themselves are not wise."

Your marriage is unique—therefore incomparable. You do not compare a Volkswagen with a Cadillac even though both of them are automobiles and both of them can take you where you want to go. Everything about these cars is different even though both of them have the same essential parts and operate on the same basic principle. The personalities and temperaments of the partners, the inherited family characteristics, the opportunities, training, and experience—these all differ widely in each situation. It is easy to imagine that other marriages are much better than yours, but you really do not know the actual state of anyone's marriage. Comparing your marriage with anyone else's can never be valid or positive. The seeds of marriage success are already in your marriage. You must water and fertilize them.

Your partner is unique. You don't need a new partner. Between you, you have the assets for building a great relationship if you are both really committed to working at it. No one else has the same potential you have—the special combination of strengths and sweetness that God has given you. All the elements for a satisfying marriage are already there if you will use them. You don't need a new job, a new outside lover, a new face-lift. All of this is right within your grasp if each of you gets a new attitude. These riches are within your reach. But you must reach for them and keep on reaching.

This will not be easy. No great marriage just happens. Anything worthwhile is worth working for. If you are facing difficulty, the tendency is to focus on the problems and see no solutions. The situation takes courage and it takes persistence, determination, commitment. Instead of comparing your marriage with others, you compare it with your own God-given potential and God's eternal workable principles. We forget that the so-called greener grass has to be mowed, fertilized, and watered just like your present lawn. Efforts to cultivate your own will yield greater and more lasting results than the fleeting excitement of escaping into an affair.

Don't look outside to see how others are doing. Pick up every practical idea you can from every source and creatively apply it to your relationship. Copy all the good ideas you can and experiment with them. Practice them. Copy, but don't compare. Look inside. You are standing right now on your own gold mine—your own acres of diamonds. Russell Conwell tells the incomparable story.

There once lived an ancient Persian by the name of Ali Hafed. He owned a very large farm, orchards, grain fields, gardens. He had many investments and was wealthy and contented. One day he was visited by an ancient Buddhist priest, a wise man of sorts. They sat by the fire and the priest recounted the detailed history of creation. He concluded by saying diamonds were the most rare and valuable gems created, "congealed drops of sunlight," and if Ali had diamonds he could get anything he wanted for himself and his family.

Ali Hafed began to dream about diamonds—about how much they were worth. He became a poor man. He had not lost anything but he was poor because he was disconcerted and discontented because he *feared* he was poor. He said, "I want a mine of diamonds," and he lay awake nights.

One morning he decided to sell his farm and all he had and travel the world in search of diamonds. He collected his money, left his family in the care of a neighbor, and began his search. He traveled Palestine and Europe extensively and found nothing. At last, after his money was all spent and he was in rags, wretchedness, and poverty, he stood on the shore at Barcelona, Spain. A great tidal wave came rolling in, and the poor, discouraged, suffering, dying man could not resist the awful temptation to cast himself into that incoming tide. He sank, never to rise again.

The man who purchased Ali Hafed's farm led his camel to his garden brook to drink one day. As the camel put its nose into the shallow water, this new owner noticed a curious flash of light from a stone in the white sands of the stream. As he stirred up the sands with his fingers he found scores of the most beautiful gems: diamonds. This was the discovery of the most magnificent diamond mine in the history of mankind— the Golconda. The largest crown jewel diamonds in the world have come from that mine.[1]

Ali Hafed's diamonds were under his own feet but he didn't realize it.

Your marriage diamonds are in your own back yard. Don't overlook them. Don't minimize them. Mine them.

DON'T SET YOUR OWN TRAPS

Many affairs are the result of falling into your own self-made and self-baited traps. We naively grease our own slide and unconsciously do the things that set us up for a fall.

Consider first your friends. In a society where flirtation is the norm and an affair is accepted behavior, you must choose and cultivate friends carefully. Friends who treat marital infidelity lightly or tell suggestive jokes and stories are really enemies of your marriage. Avoid them. Since many affairs take place between close friends—couples who have had strong friendships together—loose sex talk breaks down the protective walls, piques the curiosity, and encourages fantasies. The more open and transparent the friendship, the more necessary to keep conversation on a high level. Many a woman has faced the double tragedy of her husband's unfaithfulness with her best friend. Without appearing self-righteous or preachy, you can always find ways to let your friends know that you consider fidelity to be very important. And, of course, your own positive actions must support this so your friends see and hear that you admire, appreciate, and love your partner. When anything is said in conversation that in any way makes light of marriage, you should respond with something positive about your own relationship. Don't let the atmosphere remain poisoned with the doubts and negativism that give marriage a bad press. Be more than a silent witness. Speak up for marriage—for your marriage.

Another trap we set for ourselves is at the office, on the job. It is no secret that many affairs are spawned in the office and that sexual favors often influence contracts and affect promotions. One attractive and very competent secretary told me how she protected herself. "I turned down all invitations for private luncheons with men in our office—and there were many of them—because I knew myself and I knew it would be difficult not to respond to the admiration of other men. I valued my marriage too much to expose myself to those risks."

You must avoid the magazines and entertainment that lower inhibitions. Take TV "soaps," for instance. It is impossible to build a great marriage and be a devotee of soap operas. Their distorted drama of romance, sexuality, infidelity, affairs, and abortions encourages comparisons, dissatisfaction. Unconsciously you begin wondering why your spouse is not like "John's other wife" or "Mary's secret husband." Such fictional comparisons are bound to result in a feeling that you're being cheated in your present marriage and that an affair would bring release from your boredom. This unrealistic fantasy increases any marriage disappointment you already feel. The disappointed expectations cause you to blame your partner for letting you down. Blaming your partner causes you to become passive in your marriage-building efforts. The result of this decreasing commitment and effort is further marital deterioration. This, then, further feeds the fantasy and sets you up for an affair. It's a vicious cycle. You cannot build a real marriage on a fantasy with imaginary characters.

Margaret Hess, a Detroit pastor's wife, has some practical suggestions for avoiding your own traps.

Draw boundaries in relationships with the opposite sex. A psychologist says he avoids scheduling a woman for his last appointment. A minister keeps a counselee on the other side of a desk and keeps the drapes open. A doctor calls a nurse into the room when he must examine a woman patient. A boss and secretary can avoid going to dinner as a twosome or working evenings alone. A homemaker can avoid tempting situations with neighbors when her husband is out of town. A smart wife won't spend three months at a cottage leaving her husband to fend for himself. Neither will she look after the husband of some other wife who has gone away for the summer. Nor need a husband show undue solicitude for a wife whose husband must be away on business. She needs to feel a gap that only her husband can fill.

Mrs. Hess continues.

Do such boundaries mean avoiding warm relationships between men and women? Of course not. The Bible gives us the model. Paul advised Timothy to regard 'an elder . . . as a father; and the younger men as brothers; the older women as mothers; the younger as sisters.'[2] You can enjoy warm relationships with the opposite sex. The brother-sister relation includes identification. It expresses concern and shows love. It includes caring and even touching under some circumstances. A warm handclasp can express support. But avoid any physical contact that carries overtones of sexual attraction. What boundaries you set will depend on the amount of electricity.[3]

"Abstain from all appearance of evil."[4]

Dr. Carlfred B. Broderick sums it up in another way. "If you find yourself in a situation involving delicious privacy with an attractive member of the opposite sex, you should begin to look for ways to restructure the situation."[5] If you do not, your foot will be caught in your own net.

REFUSE TO SAW THE SAWDUST

Sawdust cannot be re-sawn. The old cud cannot be re-chewed endlessly. The past is now history and cannot be relived. You can do nothing about past behavior but learn from it. You can only live in the present moment; any reminders from yourself or others of the mistakes of the past will only victimize you and render you incapable of acting now. Refuse to let your marriage today be hurt by what used to be.

Everyone has an imperfect past. No one has an untarnished record and looks back upon an unbroken succession of victories. Everyone's past includes difficulties, disappointments, failures, and sins. No life or marriage has been all sunshine without storm, danger, or crisis.

Some look back on a failure in their home training. In fact, everyone does, because there are no perfect parents. No person gets enough fathering from his father, enough mothering from his mother, enough family-ing from the rest of the family. No marriage has been the perfect model for the children. Some of us have been deprived, gotten started wrong, come out of a broken home, learned little of love. Some experience guilt because of personal failure. Failure in business, school, morals, marriage.

Everyone has an irrevocable past. What is done is done. It can never be changed or recalled. Lord Byron, the English poet, once wrote, "No hand can make the clock strike for me the hours that are past."

No amount of effort can recall the stone already thrown.

No amount of regret can retract the hurtful words once spoken.

No amount of sorrow can undo the damage an affair does to your marriage.

No amount of tears can change the adultery into an act of purity.

No amount of apologizing will reform the act of neglect.

No pen can unwrite what has already been written.

There is no way to put that spilled milk back into the bottle—to gather up again the water lost upon the ground.

No one can possibly gather again the feathers that have been blown by the wind to only God knows where.

No amount of prayer or pious living is going to undo the damage caused by undisciplined actions and indulgence.

Your past can benefit your marriage or it will blight it. You can learn from it, build on it, and give it to God—or you can park by it, rehearse it, and be seduced by it. The past is a bully who will keep you in fear and render you impotent for the opportunities of your marriage today. Or it becomes a scapegoat so there's always somewhere to place the blame for your unwillingness to change and build your marriage now. You can develop insight into yourself by examining your past. But the insight itself will not change the past or the present.

When you excuse yourself because of your past, you are consigning yourself to mediocrity forever—always to be victimized. As Dr. Wayne W. Dyer suggests succinctly, "If my past is at fault for what I am today and the past cannot be changed, I am doomed to stay as I am."[6] There is a sign by your past that says NO PARKING HERE. If you ignore that sign, dwell on your past, review it in detail, you are indicating "My future is behind me." This then undercuts your marriage growth today and tomorrow.

The baggage from yesterday makes too big a load for today. I have traveled constantly for thirty-eight years. If I insisted on including in my luggage today every suit and shirt, every pair of shoes and socks, every suitcase from all that time, I wouldn't be able to handle it. They wouldn't let me on the airplane. It would serve no useful purpose. I have discarded all that is of no use to me today. Paul the apostle said it well for every marriage: ". . . but one thing I do: forgetting what lies behind and reaching forward to what lies ahead. . . ."[7] Each marriage partner must make and articulate just such a decision. "I will never bring up the past again. We must never let anything behind us control the future of our marriage. I will never drag any skeleton out of the closet to remind you of a past mistake, nor hold anything over you to victimize you and continue the hurt we have both suffered. The best days of our marriage are ahead of us and we will move into them and embrace them together."

Love keeps no score of suffered wrongs. You throw away the score book and get rid of your weapons of manipulation. Surrender your ace in the hole.

In this way, each day is a new beginning, not just a rehash of the past. You choose to forgive, to learn from mistakes, and to grow together. As God, upon our confession, buries our sins in the sea of His forgetfulness and never brings them against us again, He then ". . . protects us from behind."[8] Each partner must make a strong commitment to "protect the other from behind," from the self-crippling memories of the past. Remember, yesterday ended last night.

LOOK THROUGH YOUR PARTNER'S GLASSES

Because of the many temperamental and emotional differences of men and women, it is natural that they will judge their marriage differently. One partner may be receiving most of what he wants while the other is disappointed. What may be an ideal arrangement for one is boredom for the other. So, in considering the state of your marriage you must courageously ask how your partner feels, not just how you feel. Since marriage is a partnership, its condition and success must be judged by both partners. You cannot assume you both feel the same way and that because your needs are met, your spouse's are, too.

Tom and Jan are special friends of mine in Texas. As we sat around the kitchen table recently, they told me their experience. They had just gone to bed one night. Tom had kind of spread out lying on his back while they were recounting the experiences of the day. With hands behind his head he exclaimed with great satisfaction, "I am supremely happy. We have a great marriage and family, I'm doing well in business, we're in a wonderful church. I don't know how I could be more content." While he was basking in this euphoria of contentment, he realized Jan was very quiet, then the bed began to shake. Muffled sobs came from the other side of the bed and Jan broke out weeping. Tom was shocked, then got the surprise of his life when she cried, "How can you say that? I have never been so unhappy and disappointed. Nothing is going right. Everything is a mess." Tom told me, "I couldn't believe it. Couldn't understand it."

Men are often obtuse. The average husband feels that if there are no open conflicts for several weeks, no knock-downs, no thrown plates, things are going along pretty well and the marriage is in good shape. His wife may be suffering inwardly because she feels that she's taken for granted, is not understood, and that the romance has faded.

One woman who had been visiting a counselor for several months finally summoned the courage to tell her husband. His mouth dropped open as if to say, "What on earth is wrong with you?" A team of horses could not drag him to the counselor. The marriage was going splendidly—for him.

Couples often unconsciously feel that to discuss marriage needs openly will create a strain and magnify problems and that it is better to let well enough alone—let sleeping dogs lie. Don't bring the boogie-man into the light. But the opposite is true. While we assume everything is lovely, if we do not know where the fault lines are, an earthquake can be brewing and could blow everything to kingdom come. We must know the strengths and weaknesses of our partnership. We must know how our spouse feels about the quality of the marriage. The secrets must be shared while we are able to face them positively together.

Just recently I discussed their marriage with a couple who had been married for forty years. Though well-known Christians, they had not really leveled with each other all these years and each one was assuming that everything was right with the other. They both played certain roles and publicly supported each other, but in secret the wife felt she had no identity of her own and was being neglected all this time. Now it has all come out like an explosion and the pieces are scattered everywhere. She says, "Our marriage is doomed."

Ask your partner now, "How do *you* really feel about our marriage? Where do you see areas of need?" In fact, while writing this chapter at home, I left my study, went to the kitchen, and asked my wife these questions. If she is bored, I need to know it. If she is hurting, I need to know why. If she feels neglected physically, socially, sexually, I need to know that or there can be no improvement.

So ask the question and tell the truth when you answer it. Speak the truth in love about yourself, not your partner. Don't point any fingers or make accusations. Just tell how you feel. Exchange glasses for a bit so each partner gets the more accurate and balanced view. "Lovingly follow the truth at all times—speaking truly, dealing truly, living truly—and so become more and more in every way like Christ."[9]

In a growing marriage neither partner should be able to say in surprise, "But I didn't know you really felt that way."

KEEP YOUR HANDS EMPTY, BUT THE BOX FULL

Since I conduct large seminars on marriage and family life, I'm always looking for fresh titles for lectures that will have an appeal to the public. What do you think of this one? "*Ten Secret Ways To Hold Your Partner!*" I daresay that topic would be very attractive and help increase the crowd. But that would be tragic. How unfair of anyone to try to *hold* another. Instead, we need to learn ten ways to pry open the clenched fist with which each clutches the other.

We possessively hold our partner because we consistently keep the box empty. Dr. Willard Beecher tells how most people come to marriage believing it is a box full of goodies from which we extract all we need to make us happy. The marriage license is also the key to this box. We can take from it as much as we want and it somehow mysteriously remains full. And even when the box does get empty and the marriage collapses in a heap, we have not learned our lesson. We still look for a second partner that will bring another bottomless box with him so we can empty it.[10]

Marriage is an empty box. There's nothing in it. It is an opportunity to put something in, to do something for marriage. Marriage was never intended to do anything for anybody. People are expected to do something for marriage. If you do not put into the box more than you take out, it becomes empty. Love isn't in marriage, it is in people, and people put it into marriage. Romance, consideration, generosity aren't in marriage, they are in people, and people put them into the marriage box. When the box gets empty we become vulnerable for an affair.

If you intend to keep the box full you can open your hands and release the controlling grip on your partner. Holding your partner often amounts to holding your partner down. Keeping your partner really means keeping your partner controlled. This is done in several ways, for instance, by being authoritarian, bossy, domineering. This kind of husband or wife is usually married to a "weak sister," someone with a poor self-image. A leaner—one who is afraid and will do what he or she is told. A man I know treats his wife like a dog. No, he treats his dog better. He talks to his dog more than he talks to his wife, and he doesn't deceive his dog the way he's deceiving his wife with his affairs. Because she's frightened, insecure, persecution prone, she thinks it is her Christian duty to say nothing and do nothing. So he continues his bullying, tightening his grip, and she knuckles under. For fear of an uncertain future, she's cravenly holding on to him. They are both clinging for different reasons. Fists closed. Leaners.

This closed-hand possessiveness shows itself also in an inability to reinforce our partner's gifts, talents, qualities. Wives whose husbands do not encourage them to grow and develop their God-given talents are open game for the extreme voices of the women's movement. Sometimes the husband is stretched and stimulated by his work and his contacts, while his wife's mind is turning to putty with the children at home.

He controls and limits her development, then years later he turns to a sharper woman because his wife hasn't grown. Just this week in Oklahoma a daughter told me about her parents. The father, a pastor, totally neglected her mother for years, holding her down and favoring the daughter. The wife was the seldom seen, always silent partner. And he was always quoting twisted Bible verses to prove his clenched-fist policy. In time the wife and daughter both discovered they were being victimized and manipulated against each other. They have both found their own identity in Christ, were released, and are now growing usefully and developing God-given abilities. When he saw that his little game was exposed, the pastor moved out and is still quoting his verses.

Keeping an open hand means you live *for* your partner but not *through* him. David Wilkerson says to housewives:

Step out of your bondage of living your life only through others. God never intended that you find happiness only through your husband or your children. I'm not suggesting that you forsake them—only that you forsake your degrading bondage to the idea that your happiness depends only on other people. God wants you to discover a life of true happiness and contentment based only on what you are as a person and not on the moods and whims of people around you.[11]

God wants you to find your own personal identity in His creation of you and His redemption for you. You have value from birth and then you get a right standing with God and His righteousness when you receive Christ as Lord and Savior. So, whether you are husband or wife, you must have a personal and growing relationship with God that is not dependent on your partner or on your role in the family. You are free then to live *for* each other instead of *through* each other. Living through each other encourages holding on, a closed fist so you will not be let down or disappointed. Living for each other releases both of you to relax your grip and together work productively to keep the box filled.

There is a quaint little Pennsylvania Dutch restaurant in a nearby suburb where Evelyn and I like to eat. There's nothing like it in the entire Chicagoland area. The food is superb— unusual variety, deliciously flavored, enticingly prepared, large portions. When we have house guests this is the first place we think of taking them. And they always rave about it and remember it. There is no fancy decor; in fact, it is quite plain with crowded seating and oilcloth on the tables. No reservations are taken, so we usually have to wait. Not once have the owners cornered us and made us promise that we would return. Not once have they chained us to the tables to make sure we wouldn't leave them. Not once have they cried and whined, "What will we ever do if you do not come back? Don't you see what you're doing to us? How can we live without you?" Not once have they sent out goon-squads to drag customers in. And they have no discount prices. They just keep their box appetizingly full and their generous hands empty. Every customer is willing to wait patiently for a table and put up with the crowded conditions. He knows he cannot get a better deal anywhere else.

To say it another way, open the cage but keep the quality birdseed in the feeder.

BECOME THE HOST, NOT THE GUEST

Children should not be allowed to get married. If that were a law it would eliminate all marriages, since we all act like selfish children much of the time. The fact that we've committed the adult act of getting married does not make us adult. And this is the real problem underlying every other marriage difficulty. A child fills a passive/receptive role. He expects to be served. Everything is done for him. He feels no sense of responsibility or initiative. He's treated as a guest. Children do not know how to be hosts.

Any husband or wife with just a trace of honesty would admit that it's nicer to be a guest, to be enriched, entertained, pampered. To feel no sense of responsibility, to assume no expense, to sacrifice no time to prepare—just to relax, indulge, enjoy. If each of the two partners in marriage is hoping to be a guest, expecting the other to exercise initiative for his or her benefit, there is trouble. Both will be disappointed. The marriage comes to a grinding halt and an affair becomes attractive. Both begin to believe that somewhere there is someone else who will put on the show and let them be the spectator.

This is quite the opposite of what Jesus said and demonstrated. "Whoever wishes to become great among you shall be your servant; and whoever wishes to be first among you shall be slave of all. For even the Son of Man did not come to be served but to serve and give His life a ransom for many."[12] He came to be the host to serve—not the guest to be served.

No marriage can accommodate two guests—not even one guest. A satisfying marriage must have two hosts, each one personally committed to the active/initiative role of the mature adult, not the passive/receptive role of the spoiled child. Evelyn and I have entertained many hundreds of guests in our home through the years. My wife loves people, and for thirty years there was hardly a week without guests. If we went a few days with only our family, one of our sons would ask, "When are we going to have some more company?" We hosted the rich and the poor, well-known world personalities and lonely widows, famous Christian leaders and the struggling unchurched couple down the street. There were scores of luncheons, dinners, parties, large and small. Sometimes back-to-back. To be a gracious and successful host involves exactly what is needed in building a satisfying marriage.

The Host Initiates and Builds Friendships.

Generally, when guests are invited for a meal or social evening, they are friends of the host. Total strangers or enemies are not usually on your guest list. One of the objectives of the hospitality is to develop new friendships and deepen old ones. In fact, friends and friendship are the central and crucial element and as Solomon says, "A man that hath friends must show himself friendly."

Each partner in marriage should desire to say, "My spouse is my best friend." At a recent party, a Christian leader and his wife were celebrating their twenty-fifth wedding anniversary. I asked them the outstanding characteristic of their marriage. The wife answered immediately, "We have become very good friends." That is significant. You can have a compatible sex relationship and not be close friends. You can be partners in your parenting responsibilities and not enjoy an intimacy and openness as friends. You can fill your biblically prescribed roles and not accept each other as equals, which is the basis of real friendship.

The very word *friendship*, says Dr. Allan Fromme, originated in a verb of the ancient Teutonic tribal languages, meaning *to love*. In the subtle way that language has of linking related human experience, "friend" and "love" seem to have a common origin.[13] In a survey of more than 40,000 Americans conducted by *Psychology Today* these qualities were most valued in a friend: the ability to keep confidences, loyalty, warmth, and affection. In his book *Love Life*, my friend Dr. Ed Wheat has a great chapter on becoming best friends. I strongly recommend it. The beginning of friendship love *(phileo),* he says, is "We spend time together, we have fun together, we share activities and interests, we know and like each other, we talk things over, we confide in each other, we call on each other for help, we count on each other's loyalty. Shared time, shared activities, shared interests, and shared experiences lead to shared feelings and shared confidences." "This was the cream of our marriage," Jan Struther said. "This nightly turning out and sharing of the day's pocketfull of memories."[14]

Assuming the role of the host we would treat our partners the way we treat our guests. Suppose a guest accidentally spills coffee on your fine tablecloth. How do you react? "Think nothing of it. We do it ourselves all the time. Here, let me help you wipe it up so you don't get it on your clothes." Your husband does the same. "You are so clumsy. Why can't you be more careful? You ruined my best tablecloth. You don't care how much time I have to spend cleaning up after you."

We often show friends kindness, consideration, courtesy. This prompts one important question. "How would I act if this happened to a guest in my home?" Ask this when your wife dents the car, when your husband ruins the carpet or drops the china, when your favorite vase is broken, and all things both more and less serious. Picture your partner as your invited guest and speak accordingly. The better your friend, the more necessary do tact and courtesy become.

The Host Is Also a Careful Planner.
Accomplished hosts/hostesses do not get that way by accident. They plan their events down to the last detail. Nothing is taken for granted. The party that comes off so smoothly and efficiently is really the result of much thought, time, and expense. My wife is having a small luncheon tomorrow and already I've seen the preparations for it. Special seashells for the tuna salad, things in the refrigerator I cannot sample,

notes that remind her of small but important details. And she has talked about this luncheon every day for at least the past week.

Marriages without that same kind of careful effort and thoughtful planning will decay. The most destructive notion that marriage partners have about marriage is that it will somehow roll along on its own momentum. However, the natural tendency is to drift apart, not to grow together. Uncultivated ground grows weeds, not flowers. Laziness and lack of initiative pave the way for boredom and the temptation to look elsewhere. Good times do not just happen. A love note in the lunchbox or under the pillow does not appear by magic. A meal seasoned with love is not already store-packaged. For a candlelight dinner someone has to light the candles. For a weekend alone someone has to make the reservations. Love must be planned. Courtship must be cultivated. Love will grow or die. Someone must think, think, think. An intimate long-term marriage, says W. H. Auden, "is not the involuntary result of fleeting emotion but the creation of time and will." If you plan for things to happen, they will.

The Host Considerately Meets Needs.

He takes responsibility for the comfort of his guests. Music creates a relaxing atmosphere, comfortable seating is provided, appetizers and hors d'oeuvres are served. Finally, a full course meal is provided. The host makes sure the room temperature is right. Conversation is initiated and strangers are introduced so that all the guests feel at ease. He is committed to meeting their social needs.

Get a firm picture in your mind of yourself as the host and your spouse as the guest. Do you see it? You—attentive, caring, considerate, generous, an initiator. Now, how would you meet your spouse's *emotional needs?* Would you be able to carve out some quality time together? To talk about your mutual interests? To share each other's goals and dreams? One mother whispered to her daughter just before she was to walk down the aisle in her wedding, "Now you'll know what real loneliness is."

What about *sexual needs?* How would you go about meeting your partner's sexual needs if you were the host? Would you be more sensitive? More generous? More creative? Less excusing and blaming? Would you not learn all you could about your partner's sexual nature? Would you remain in ignorance? The spouse who refuses to be the host and provide for his or her partner's sexual satisfaction is just begging for someone else to stand in and meet the need.

Spiritual needs? If you assumed responsibility for your partner's spiritual development would you become more familiar with the Bible? More aware of how to pray together and encourage one another?

Supper was over. Their sweaty bodies were relaxing and their tired feet still spoke of the hot dusty roads they had traveled. The disciples were in a reflective mood, rehearsing what they had seen and heard on that special Jewish holiday called the Passover. Jesus had taught some startling things that day, mind-blowing things like "When you see me you are seeing the One who sent me." Dozens of statements like that.

During a lull in the conversation Jesus stood and removed his robe. Out of a deep sense of where He came from, who He was, and what He had, He wrapped a towel around His waist, poured some water in a basin and began to wash these disciples' feet. Their leader became their servant. Shocking! He was the host. They were the guests. He had met their human needs for food and camaraderie and now was talking to them of partnership, service, and love. *The Living Bible* translates John 13:3, "And how he loved his disciples." Then

He said, "I have given you an example to follow: do as I have done to you." That's what it takes to be the host, He says: great love and humble serving.

Again, in the early morning darkness after His resurrection Jesus stood by the Sea of Tiberias waiting for seven of His disciples. When their boat came within the sound of His voice, He invited them for breakfast. "Be my guests," He said. They were tired, discouraged after fishing all night and catching nothing. He suggested that they cast their net on the opposite side of the boat, and their nets were suddenly filled. He had prepared a fire for their chill, food for their hunger, and encouragement in their task. And He talked with them about friendship, love, and following Him. When the meal was over they left with joy and hope, their needs met. He was the perfect host.

ACTIVATE LOVE BY YOUR ACTIONS

"Love is the only emotion that isn't natural. The only one that has to be learned and the only one that matters. Real love is a skill rarely learned before the age of thirty-five. No love, not even maternal love, is instinctive or innate. Most people can love only in shabby, suspicious amounts: when they speak of love they mean getting it, not giving it."[15] Canadian author June Callwood is right on target. Love has to be learned. Love is a skill. Love involves giving. Though love is the most desired commodity in the world and uncounted volumes have been written extolling and explaining it, yet we still have so little of it and so little understanding of how it works. William Penn acknowledged it to be the hardest lesson in Christianity.

It is a sad commentary on our whole society that we are more familiar with the romantic type of love that traffics in mascara, moon-June music, mouthwash, and padded bras. And we continue to exalt it without calling it what it really is—a child's world of wishful thinking. André Maurois put it more crassly when he reflected with disgust, "We owe to the middle ages the two worst inventions of humanity—romantic love and gunpowder."

The misconceptions of love persist. To many it is a right to be pampered. A debt others owe—a guarantee. You have fallen in love and now that you are married you can fold your arms and wait for marriage to deliver the happiness that is yours by contract. You get love by giving it, not demanding it. It is a myth that love is automatically present and will somehow surface sooner or later. If you believe this, disappointment is inevitable.

Related to this is the notion that love *happens* to you. Your choice or action is secondary and you become a wonderful victim of love. Or that love is some kind of deposit you receive at birth that makes up a reservoir from which you can draw at will, to meet your needs and others'. Or that we come equipped with a fixed, finite ability to love—a special talent. We often see ourselves as understanding, giving, and generally loving, even though the facts fail to support such a handsome picture of ourselves. But we believe that love is a passive emotion that lives and dies inside of us, and that comes and goes depending on luck, providence, or favorable circumstances.

In the words of Katherine Ann Porter, "Love must be learned, and learned again, and again; there is no end to it." June Callwood agrees. "A life without love, according to modern psychologists, is a life of destruction and insanity. And while anger, hate, and guilt bloom in the bassinette, love, sympathy and tact require decades of study and tutelage."[16]

To learn, we must study. And the Bible, by the way, is the only authoritative and completely accurate source book on love to be found anywhere. There are three major passages in the Bible that deal with love, its elements and its practice. The Song of Solomon is a detailed and candid story of wedded love. 1 Corinthians 13 is a chapter showing what love is made of and how it behaves. 1 John 3 and 4 stress the twin truths that love must first be received from God and then actively given to others. In these two chapters, the verbs *doing, practice, giving, acting, loving* are used repeatedly. Since love is commanded by God—husbands love your wives, let us practice loving—this shows that love is a choice. God cannot command our feelings or emotions. We cannot either. God's injunction can be obeyed only if loving is a decision we choose, an action we initiate. In fact, it is a choice expressed in action and backed up by action. This is why God says, "Let us stop just *saying* we love people; let us *really* love them, and *show* it by our *actions*." Therefore, as we've said in an earlier chapter, love is something you do. This takes the mystery and the myth out of it—the cheap sentimentality and the irrationality. Love is an art that is learned and a discipline that is practiced. The attention and effort that go into mastering any art, skill, or vocation must be committed to learning to love. This involves discipline, concentration, patience, and commitment. Since these love actions are a matter of choice, they are not dependent on our feelings. In fact, they may be contrary to our feelings. Just yesterday a wife told me, "I no longer have any feeling for my husband. I cannot touch him and I don't want him to touch me. And you want me to reach out to him when I feel this way?" Exactly! The repeated positive action can have a positive effect on your feelings.

To repeat the principles from chapter four, "We do not do what we do because we feel the way we feel. We feel the way we feel because we do what we do." Hypocrisy, you say! "You want me to speak love, express love, demonstrate love when I don't feel like it?" a husband queried. Absolutely. Act "as if." It would be hypocrisy only if your motive were to deceive or manipulate your partner. If your desire is to build a relationship and practice God's truth, God will honor it and the right feelings will follow.

Newspaper columnist and minister Dr. George Crane tells this enlightening experience. A wife came into his office full of hatred toward her husband and committed to getting a divorce. "I do not only want to get rid of him, I want to get even with him. Before I divorce him I want to hurt him as much as I can because of what he has done to me." Dr. Crane suggested an ingenious plan. "Go home and think and act as if you really loved your husband. Tell him how much he means to you. Admire all his good qualities; praise him for every decent trait. Go out of your way to be as kind, considerate, and generous as possible. Spare no efforts to give of yourself to him in every way, to please him, to enjoy him. Do everything you can possibly think of to make him believe you love him. After you've convinced him of your undying love and that you cannot live without him, *then* drop the bomb. Tell him how much you hate him and that you're getting a divorce. That will really hurt him."

With revenge in her eyes, she smiled and exclaimed, "Beautiful, beautiful. Will he ever be surprised!"

And she did it, with enthusiasm. Acting "as if." For two months she initiated love actions, kindness, listening, giving, reinforcing, sharing, "doing the very best for the object of one's love."

When she didn't return, Dr. Crane called. "Are you ready now to go through with the divorce?"

"Divorce?" she exclaimed. "Never! I discovered I really do love him." Her actions had changed her feelings. Motion resulted in emotion. The experiment became an experience.

Dr. Ed Wheat sums it up in these four principles. "One, I can learn what love is from the Word of God and grow in my understanding of it. Two, love is not easy or simple—it is an art I must learn and pour myself into. Three, love is an active power I control by my own will. I can choose to love. Four, love is the power that will produce love as I learn to give it, rather than strain to attract it."[17]

Your ability to love is established not so much by fervent promise as often repeated deeds. "And when we love each other God lives in us and His love within us grows ever stronger." The thrilling truth is that as you give love to others God gives more love to you. You become a conduit, not a cistern. Your supply of His love is increased as you activate love by your actions. When you stop loving, you short-change yourself. The source dries up. Henry Drummond, the famous author on the subject of love, summarizes it all.

Is life not full of opportunities for learning to love? Every man and woman every day has thousands of them. The world is not a playground; it's a schoolroom. Life is not a holiday, but an education. And the one eternal lesson for us all is how better we can love. What makes a man a good artist, a good sculptor, a good musician? Practice. What makes a man a good man? Practice. Love is not a thing of enthusiastic emotion. It is a rich, strong, manly, vigorous expression of the whole Christian character—the Christ-like nature in its fullest development. And the constituents of this great character are only to be built up by ceaseless practice.[18]

START YOUR OWN AFFAIR AT HOME

"Affairs are, and will be because people want satisfying, qualitative couple relationships, and if they don't find them in their marriages, they'll look for them elsewhere. The urges underlying affairs are deeply human and active in us all." That statement comes from Dr. Tom McGinnis, a counseling psychologist in Fair Lawn, New Jersey.

If there's any truth in his assertion, then it follows that by providing at home what the affair promises, the temptation to the affair is rendered impotent. What are the elements in an affair that make it attractive? What does it offer? What are its unspoken secrets and mysteries? What is its challenge to a jaded marriage? What are the qualities you can build into your marriage that will give you the "feelings" an affair provides without the deception, destruction, and guilt that an affair inevitably produces?

The most descriptive thing I've read about what necessities a marriage must offer to counter-attack the appeal of an affair comes from Dr. McGinnis, mentioned above. It is quoted by Nicki McWhirter of Knight-Ridder News Service.

Married people seek out or succumb to affairs when they feel devalued and less than fully alive. They are bored. Over-burdened. It amounts to being very lonely, and it can happen in a household full of kids and babbling spouse in which there is a back-breaking schedule of "fun" things to do.

People who have affairs have the child's deep longing to be touched, caressed, held, hugged and kissed, whether they can admit it or not. They want happy surprises. That might mean a sentimental, unexpected gift every once in a while. More important, it is the dependable gift of time and caring, the present of shared ideas, experiences, stories, nonsense, and games, including sexual games. They want the world to butt out.

They want a loving friend, a pal who isn't judgmental. They want someone to convince them they're still loved, lovable, and very special. For a little while, now and then, they want out from under the grown-up responsibilities that have become predictable, dreary and difficult.

There are at least seventeen separate thoughts, qualities,

characteristics mentioned here. I have isolated each of these important ideas and posed three questions about each one. Go over these questions carefully. Consider them thoughtfully. Answer them honestly. Your honest answers can forecast a new beginning—can be a change-point. They will indicate where you can begin to change the climate of your marriage and create the situations that will give you and your partner the good feelings you need. (I have also included these questions on separate pages at the end of this chapter so you can remove them and keep them before you while these new habits are being formed.)

One last, important question. Is it really possible to build and maintain a vibrant marriage? Can we face the inevitable disappointments and conflicts with courage and grow in love and intimacy? The answer is yes, emphatically YES. Another triangle is involved. You, your partner, and God. Each one is indispensable to the success of the marriage. God will not do your part—you cannot do His. It is a partnership. A personal relationship with God enables you to bring your best to the marriage. He then adds the extra dimension of love, peace, joy, strength, and forgiveness that you cannot create yourself.

God is who He says He is. You are who He says you are. God will do what He says He will do. You can do what He says you should do.

I have learned in any and all circumstances the secret of facing every situation, whether well fed or going hungry, having a sufficiency to spare or going without and being in want.

I have strength for all things in Christ who empowers me— I am ready for anything and equal to anything through Him who infuses inner strength to me. I am self-sufficient in Christ's sufficiency.[19]

THREE FINAL THOUGHTS

"One thing remains unchanged through the centuries: nothing is finer, more fulfilling—indeed, more sanctified—than the inviolate marriage bed, particularly when the decision that it will remain inviolate is the conscious act of the two people who share it."[20]

"There is a vast difference between wanting something when we do not have it and continuing to want it when we do have it. Continuing to desire and cherish what we have means that we have established a relationship, that we have formed an attachment—that we do, in fact, love."[21]

More than a century ago, Henry David Thoreau said it succinctly. "Simplify, simplify, simplify." Focus on, and stay true to, what is at the center, and like planets around the sun of our marriage, the other elements of life will find their right places. Be faithful, stay faithful, have faith—and happiness will happen.

A Marriage Test
for Wives and
Husbands

MARRIAGE TEST FOR WIVES

	Never	Occasionally	Frequently
Unappreciated			
I consider my husband a person of worth and listen with eye contact and focused attention.	____	____	____
I take my husband for granted and forget to notice and praise him.	____	____	____
I support my husband in times of failure with reassurance and affirmation.	____	____	____
Lifeless			
I encourage my husband to think and feel young.	____	____	____
I plan things we can do together that encourage romance.	____	____	____
I resist creative changes that could add spice and variety to our lives.	____	____	____
Bored			
I consider my marriage a dreary routine.	____	____	____
I have growing expectations, plans, and goals for our marriage.	____	____	____
I encourage my husband to develop his talents, hobbies, qualities, and gifts.	____	____	____
Overburdened			
I am critical of my husband because of financial problems and differences.	____	____	____
I support my husband in his job (in or out of the home) and encourage his success.	____	____	____
I do not allow my parents to interfere or create tension in our marriage.	____	____	____

	Never	Occasionally	Frequently
Lonely			
I try to understand my husband's loneliness and encourage him to express it.	_____	_____	_____
I openly express my own feelings to my husband and tell him what I need.	_____	_____	_____
I am learning to open up and overcome the tendency to retreat into my shell.	_____	_____	_____
Children			
I let my husband and the children know that he is first in my affection.	_____	_____	_____
I encourage a marriage-centered, not child-centered, home.	_____	_____	_____
I give leadership to the spiritual training of our children through Bible reading and prayer.	_____	_____	_____
Schedule			
I am highly organized for each day, allowing no time for spontaneity and surprises.	_____	_____	_____
I am a slave to the urgent request of outsiders, becoming a means to their ends.	_____	_____	_____
My expectations of my husband and children cause them to feel pressured, inadequate, unable to please.	_____	_____	_____
Touching			
I find ways each day to touch and hold my husband so he knows I appreciate him.	_____	_____	_____
I enjoy the delight of caressing and hugging without insisting it culminate in sex relations.	_____	_____	_____
I keep myself inviting so my husband is not repulsed by offensive attitudes, appearance, and odors.	_____	_____	_____

Marriage Test for Wives

	Never	Occasionally	Frequently
Surprises			
I think of special or unusual things I could do for or with my husband.	____	____	____
I arrange for surprise events— eating out, entertainment, trips, weekends away.	____	____	____
I think of long-term ways to stretch my husband's interests and opportunities for growth.	____	____	____
Gifts			
I give my husband one large gift on his birthday, anniversary, and Christmas and this satisfies him all year.	____	____	____
I give small gifts on many unexpected occasions because I think of him often.	____	____	____
I usually give utilitarian gifts rather than personal ones that say to my husband, "You are specially appreciated."	____	____	____
Shared Ideas			
I have outgrown my husband and do not positively encourage his development.	____	____	____
I plan relaxing times together so we can share our dreams.	____	____	____
I discuss fully with my husband our plans for our marriage, our children, our future.	____	____	____
Laughter			
I do everything I can to make our house a fun place to come home to.	____	____	____
I encourage meal times to be special, happy times with a positive atmosphere of interaction.	____	____	____
I freely share jokes and funny stories on myself rather than on other family members.	____	____	____

	Never	Occasionally	Frequently

Sexual Games

I flirt with my husband and encourage this kind of romance and aliveness.

I take an active part in our sex life with genuine pleasure and abandon.

I am aggressive in loving my husband, seeking to delight him in every way possible and not using sex against him as a weapon, tool, or reward.

Loving Friend

I keep my husband's confidences and do not withhold from him any secrets that affect our marriage.

I am loyal to my husband and support and praise him publicly.

I encourage him in the face of difficulties or defeat and stand by him faithfully.

Acceptance

I have fully accepted my husband with all his personal traits and idiosyncrasies.

I have forgiven everything in his past and do not hold anything against him.

I enjoy my husband and feel free to open my heart to him.

Loved—Special

I have a growing desire for my husband's happiness and comfort.

I am committed to learning my husband's unique love language and practicing it.

I constantly tell my husband how special he is as a friend, partner, and lover.

Marriage Test for Wives

Dreariness	Never	Occasionally	Frequently
I nag about household chores and feel tied down and resentful.	____	_____	_____
I resent my husband's taking time for recreation, hobbies, shopping, Bible study group.	____	_____	_____
I tend to be a workaholic and feel guilty about planning special days or weekends for relaxing together.	____	_____	_____

MARRIAGE TEST FOR HUSBANDS

	Never	Occasionally	Frequently
Unappreciated			
I consider my wife a person of worth and listen with eye contact and focused attention.	____	_____	_____
I take my wife for granted and forget to notice and praise her.	____	_____	_____
I support my wife in times of failure with reassurance and affirmation.	____	_____	_____
Lifeless			
I encourage my wife to think and feel young.	____	_____	_____
I plan things we can do together that encourage romance.	____	_____	_____
I resist creative changes that could add spice and variety to our lives.	____	_____	_____
Bored			
I consider my marriage a dreary routine.	____	_____	_____
I have growing expectations, plans, and goals for our marriage.	____	_____	_____
I encourage my wife to develop her talents, hobbies, qualities, and gifts.	____	_____	_____
Overburdened			
I am critical of my wife because of financial problems and differences.	____	_____	_____
I support my wife in her job (in or out of the home) and encourage her success.	____	_____	_____
I do not allow my parents to interfere or create tension in our marriage.	____	_____	_____

	Never	Occasionally	Frequently

Lonely

I try to understand my wife's loneliness and encourage her to express it.

I openly express my own feelings to my wife and tell her what I need.

I am learning to open up and overcome the tendency to retreat into my shell.

Children

I let my wife and the children know that she is first in my affection.

I encourage a marriage-centered, not child-centered, home.

I give leadership to the spiritual training of our children through Bible reading and prayer.

Schedule

I am highly organized for each day, allowing no time for spontaneity and surprises.

I am a slave to the urgent request of outsiders, becoming a means to their ends.

My expectations of my wife and children cause them to feel pressured, inadequate, unable to please.

Touching

I find ways each day to touch and hold my wife so she knows I appreciate her.

I enjoy the delight of caressing and hugging without insisting it culminate in sex relations.

I keep myself inviting so my wife is not repulsed by offensive attitudes, appearance, and odors.

Marriage Test for Husbands

	Never	Occasionally	Frequently
Surprises			
I think of special or unusual things I could do for or with my wife.	___	___	___
I arrange for surprise events— eating out, entertainment, trips, weekends away.	___	___	___
I think of long-term ways to stretch my wife's interests and opportunities for growth.	___	___	___
Gifts			
I give my wife one large gift on her birthday, anniversary, and Christmas and this satisfies her all year.	___	___	___
I give small gifts on many unexpected occasions because I think of her often.	___	___	___
I usually give utilitarian gifts rather than personal ones that say to my wife, "You are specially appreciated."	___	___	___
Shared Ideas			
I have outgrown my wife and do not positively encourage her development.	___	___	___
I plan relaxing times together so we can share our dreams.	___	___	___
I discuss fully with my wife our plans for our marriage, our children, our future.	___	___	___
Laughter			
I do everything I can to make our house a fun place to come home to.	___	___	___
I encourage meal times to be special, happy times with a positive atmosphere of interaction.	___	___	___
I freely share jokes and funny stories on myself rather than on other family members.	___	___	___

	Never	Occasionally	Frequently

Sexual Games
I flirt with my wife and enjoy and encourage this kind of romance and aliveness.

I take an active part in our sex life with genuine pleasure and abandon.

I am aggressive in loving my wife, seeking to delight her in every way possible and not using sex against her as a weapon, tool, or reward.

Loving Friend
I keep my wife's confidences and do not withhold from her any secrets that affect our marriage.

I am loyal to my wife and support and praise her publicly.

I encourage her in the face of difficulties and defeat and stand by her faithfully.

Acceptance
I have fully accepted my wife with all her personal traits and idiosyncrasies.

I have forgiven everything in her past and do not hold anything against her.

I enjoy my wife and feel free to open my heart to her.

Loved—Special
I have a growing desire for my wife's happiness and comfort.

I am committed to learning my wife's unique love language and practicing it.

I constantly tell my wife how special she is as a friend, partner, and lover.

Marriage Test for Husbands

Dreariness	*Never*	*Occasionally*	*Frequently*
I nag about household chores and feel tied down and resentful.	____	_____	_____
I resent my wife's taking time for recreation, hobbies, shopping, Bible study group.	____	_____	_____
I tend to be a workaholic and feel guilty about planning special days or weekends for relaxing together.	____	_____	_____

N O T E S

CHAPTER 1

1. Robert A. Harper, *Extramarital Relations* (New York: Hawthorn Books, 1967), pp. 385-391.
2. Julia S. Brown, "A Comparative Study of Deviation from Sexual Mores," *The American Sociological Review* 17 (1952), pp. 135-146.
3. *Playboy* Survey, Morton Hunt, *Sexual Behavior in the 1970's* (Chicago: Playboy Press, 1974), n.p.
4. "Family Life," *American Institute of Family Relations* (January 1970), pp. 7, 8.
5. Dr. Sam Janus in *People* magazine, n.d.
6. Louis Harris Poll, 1978-79.
7. Eve Baguedor, "Is Anyone Faithful Anymore?" *McCall's* (February 1973), p. 73.
8. Alexander Lowen and Robert J. Levin, "The Case Against Cheating in Marriage," *Redbook* (June 1969). Condensed in *Reader's Digest* (November 1969).
9. Galatians 6:7, *The Jerusalem Bible.*

CHAPTER 2

Chapter Introduction. Florence Littauer, *After Every Wedding Comes a Marriage* (Eugene, Oregon: Harvest House), p. 155.

1. Roberta Kells Dorr, *David and Bathsheba* (Wheaton: Tyndale House Publishers, Inc., 1982), p. 238.
2. 2 Samuel 8:6, *The Living Bible.*
3. 2 Samuel 7:8-28, TLB.
4. 2 Samuel 6:21, TLB.
5. 2 Samuel 8:15, TLB.
6. James 1:12-16.
7. John 3:19.
8. 2 Samuel 11:15, TLB.
9. 2 Samuel 11:27, TLB.
10. 2 Samuel 18:33.

CHAPTER 3

Chapter Introduction. Susan Squire, "Extramarital Affair," *Glamour* magazine (September 1980), p. 278.

1. Linda Wolfe, "How Three Wives Justify Their Love Affairs," *Redbook* (May 1973), p. 90.
2. Proverbs 11:2, TLB.
3. 1 Timothy 3:6, TLB.
4. Proverbs 17:9; 25:24; 27:15, TLB.

5. James Dobson, "The Lure of Infidelity," a Focus on the Family tape.
6. Evelyn Miller Berger, *Triangle: The Betrayed Wife* (Chicago: Nelson-Hall Co.), p. 49.
7. John Drescher, *When Opposites Attract* (St. Meinrad, Indiana: Abbey Press, 1979), p. 31.
8. Ed Wheat, *Love Life* (Grand Rapids: Zondervan Publishers, 1980), p. 181.
9. Marabel Morgan, *Total Joy* (Old Tappan, New Jersey: Fleming H. Revell, 1976), pp. 74, 75.
10. Lou Beardsley and Toni Spry, *The Fulfilled Woman* (Eugene, Oregon: Harvest House, 1975), p. 29.
11. Ella Wheeler Wilcox, "An Unfaithful Wife to Her Husband," *Whatever Is, Is Best,* Collection of Poems (Boulder, Colorado: Blue Mountain Arts, Inc., 1975), pp. 62, 63.

CHAPTER 4
1. Genesis 24:12-19
2. Matthew 20:25-28.
3. David Wilkerson, *Have You Felt Like Giving Up Lately?* (Old Tappan, New Jersey: Fleming H. Revell, 1980), p. 35.
4. 1 John 4:7, TLB.
5. Matthew 19:5, 6.
6. Armin Grams, *Changes in Family Life* (St. Louis: Concordia Publishing Company, 1968), p. 46.
7. J. Allan Petersen, *The Marriage Affair* (Wheaton: Tyndale House Publishers, Inc., 1971), p. 125.

CHAPTER 5
Chapter Introduction. Ellen Williams, *Today's Christian Woman* (Winter 1981-1982), pp. 49-51.
1. James 1:13-15, *The Jerusalem Bible.*
2. 1 Peter 5:8, TLB.
3. Hebrews 4:15, *King James Version.*
4. "The Subtlety of Sexual Sin," *Eternity* (February 1977), p. 28.
5. Proverbs 23:7.
6. David L. Hocking, *Love and Marriage* (Eugene, Oregon: Harvest House, 1981), pp. 58, 59.
7. David Stoop, *Self-Talk* (Old Tappan, New Jersey: Fleming H. Revell, 1982), p. 33.
8. Romans 12:2.
9. Proverbs 2:16-18, *Today's English Version;* 4:23-27, TLB; 5:3, 4, TEV; 5:15-19, TLB; 6:25-32, TLB; 9:13-18, TLB; Malachi 2:15, TLB; 1 Corinthians 6:18-20, TLB; 1 Thessalonians 4:3-8, TLB; Hebrews 13:4, TLB.
10. E. Stanley Jones, *The Way to Power and Poise* (Nashville: Abingdon Press, 1949), p. 258.
11. Philippians 4:8, TLB.

12. 1 Peter 1:13, KJV.
13. Isaiah 26:3, KJV.

CHAPTER 6
1. Linda Wolfe, "The Unfaithful Husband," *Ladies Home Journal* (August 1977), pp. 130-134.
2. Ellen Williams, *Today's Christian Woman* (Winter 1982), pp. 49-51.
3. Evelyn Miller Berger, *Triangle: The Betrayed Wife,* p. 71.
4. Linda Wolfe, *Redbook* (May 1973), p. 69.
5. Evelyn Miller Berger, *Triangle: The Betrayed Wife,* p. 71.
6. Abigail Van Buren, "When Your Husband Is Unfaithful," *McCall's* (January 1963), p. 75.

CHAPTER 7
Chapter Introduction. Evelyn Miller Berger, *Triangle: The Betrayed Wife,* p. xiv.
1. Evelyn Miller Berger, *Triangle: The Betrayed Wife,* p. 170.
2. Natalie Gittelson, "Infidelity—Can You Forgive and Forget?" *Redbook* (November 1978), p. 191.
3. Ellen Williams, *Today's Christian Woman* (Winter 1982), pp. 49-51.
4. Susan Jacoby, "After His Affair," *McCall's* (February 1982), p. 120.
5. Susan Squire, "Extramarital Affair," *Glamour* (September 1980), p. 278.
6. Susan Jacoby, "After His Affair," pp. 121, 122.
7. Susan Jacoby, "After His Affair," pp. 121, 122.
8. Peter Kreitler with Bill Bruns, *Affair Prevention* (New York: Macmillan Publishing Co., Inc., 1981), pp. 16-28.
9. Natalie Gittelson, "Infidelity—Can You Forgive and Forget?" p. 191.
10. Susan Squire, "Extramarital Affair," *Glamour,* p. 280.
11. Natalie Gittelson, "Infidelity—Can You Forgive and Forget?" p. 192.
12. Natalie Gittelson, "Infidelity—Can You Forgive and Forget?" p. 192.
13. Natalie Gittelson, "Infidelity—Can You Forgive and Forget?" p. 193.
14. Henry Wildeboer, "Rebuilding Marital Fidelity," *Christianity Today* (June 18, 1971).
15. David Reuben, "Why Husbands Cheat on Their Wives," *Woman's Day* (April 1972).
16. 1 John 1:9.
17. Philippians 4:13.
18. Willard and Marguerite Beecher, *Beyond Success and Failure* (New York: The Julian Press, 1966), p. 213.
19. Natalie Gittelson, "Infidelity—Can You Forgive and Forget?" p. 191.
20. 1 Corinthians 6:18-20, *New American Standard Bible.*
21. Psalm 32:5, *Revised Standard Version.*
22. Psalm 51:4, RSV.
23. Psalm 32:2-5, TLB.
24. Mark 11:25, RSV.
25. Henry Wildeboer, "Rebuilding Marital Fidelity," *Christianity Today* (June 18, 1971).

26. Abigail Van Buren, "When Your Husband Is Unfaithful," *McCall's* (January 1963), p. 74.

CHAPTER 9

Chapter Introduction. Norman M. Lobsenz, "Make Your Marriage Affair-Proof," *Woman's Day* (March 13, 1979), p. 150.
 1. Russell Conwell, *Acres of Diamonds* (New York: Harper and Row, 1915).
 2. 1 Timothy 5:1, 2.
 3. Margaret Hess, *Moody Monthly* (March 1967), pp. 75, 76.
 4. 1 Thessalonians 5:22.
 5. Peter Kreitler with Bill Bruns, *Affair Prevention,* p. 15.
 6. Wayne W. Dyer, *Pulling Your Own Strings* (New York: Avon Books, 1978), p. 65.
 7. Philippians 3:13, NASB.
 8. Isaiah 52:12, TLB.
 9. Ephesians 4:15, 16, TLB.
10. Willard and Marguerite Beecher, *Beyond Success and Failure,* p. 108.
11. David Wilkerson, *Have You Felt Like Giving Up Lately?* p. 36.
12. Mark 10:43-45, NASB.
13. Allan Fromme, *The Ability to Love* (New York: Pocket Books, 1966), p. 175.
14. Ed Wheat, *Love Life,* pp. 50-53.
15. June Callwood, *Love, Hate, Fear, Anger* (Garden City, N.Y.: Doubleday, 1964), p. 1.
16. June Callwood, *Love, Hate, Fear, Anger,* p. 3.
17. Ed Wheat, *Love Life,* pp. 50-53.
18. Henry Drummond, *The Greatest Thing in the World* (Old Tappan, New Jersey: Fleming H. Revell, Spire Edition, 1968), pp. 39-41.
19. Philippians 4:12, 13, *The Amplified Bible.*
20. Natalie Gittelson, "Unfaithful Wives: What Happens to Their Marriages," *McCall's* (June 1980), p. 26.
21. Allan Fromme, *The Ability to Love,* p. 298.